T0368361

WINDPROOF

F. Austin DeLoach Jr.

WestBow
PRESS®
A DIVISION OF THOMAS NELSON
& ZONDERVAN

WestBow Press books may be ordered through booksellers or by contacting:

WestBow Press
A Division of Thomas Nelson & Zondervan
1663 Liberty Drive
Bloomington, IN 47403
www.westbowpress.com
844-714-3454

Scripture quotations marked NKJV are taken from the New King James Version. Copyright © 1982 by Thomas Nelson, Inc. Used by permission. All rights reserved.

Scripture quotations marked NLT are taken from the Holy Bible, New Living Translation, copyright © 1996, 2004, 2007 by Tyndale House Foundation. Used by permission of Tyndale House Publishers, Inc., Carol Stream, Illinois 60188. All rights reserved.

Scripture quotations marked NASB are taken from the New American Standard Bible®, Copyright © 1960, 1962, 1963, 1968, 1971, 1972, 1973, 1975, 1977, 1995 by The Lockman Foundation. Used by permission.

ISBN: 979-8-3850-3484-0 (sc)
ISBN: 979-8-3850-3486-4 (hc)
ISBN: 979-8-3850-3485-7 (e)

Library of Congress Control Number: 2024920419

Print information available on the last page.

WestBow Press rev. date: 04/10/2025

CONTENTS

CONTENTS

ACKNOWLEDGEMENTS

This book would not have come together without the support and efforts of some incredible individuals. First, I want to express my deep gratitude to Tim Watson, Mary Lou Thornton, Traci Jones, and Janice Daugharty for their keen editorial eyes and thoughtful guidance. Your dedication to refining this work has been invaluable.

A heartfelt thank you to Justin and Laurie Roberts for providing me the time and space to retreat and focus on finishing this book. Your generosity and encouragement allowed me to see this project through to completion.

To all who have supported and encouraged me along the way—thank you, especially the amazing people *at* Cornerstone and TruthPoint. *Your* constant love and support give me strength and inspiration.

DEDICATION

To my wife, Jennifer—your unwavering love, strength, and encouragement are a constant blessing in my life and an inspiration to many others. I am endlessly grateful for you.

To my daughters, KenLee and Dempsey Anna, your presence fills my days with joy and reminds me of life's beauty and blessings.

To my daughter Alora Gail and her husband, Bran—may your shared journey be one of love, faith, and countless blessings.

To Aunt Donna – whose love for God's Word still inspires me. You made an indelible mark on this world.

And to my Mama and Daddy—thank you for instilling in me a love for truth.

This book is dedicated to all of you with deep gratitude.

And thank you, Jesus, from whom all good and perfect gifts come!

INTRODUCTION

The words to an old hymn come to mind as I prepare you to read this book:

> My hope is built on nothing less
> than Jesus's blood and righteousness;
> I dare not trust the sweetest frame,
> but wholly lean on Jesus's name.
>
> On Christ, the solid Rock, I stand;
> All other ground is sinking sand,
> All other ground is sinking sand.

As a teenager, I probably mumbled these words with little thought and enthusiasm. With time and life experiences, however, I realized I had constructed my life on sand. The world offers nothing for stability on this sin-stricken, shaky planet. But Jesus does.

The year 2020 was a vivid reminder of why the theme of this book is essential. COVID-19 rocked the world. The virus was like the stormy weather Jesus spoke of in Matthew 7:24–28. The wind came and went relatively quickly but revealed a lot. We were collectively and individually reminded of how quickly things around us can change. Churches were unable to gather. The hallways of schools were hollow for months. Fear took over the nation's soul. Masks and social distancing were mandated and brought division, even among churches. All of this (and much more) reminded us of the truth of Jesus's words: We will all face fierce wind and heavy rain in life.

A teaching of Jesus, commonly called the Sermon on the Mount, covers a range of topics: happiness, anger, adultery, love, prayer, money, and worry. What was it like to hear God, wrapped in flesh, teach on the mountainside that day? As the Master Teacher, Jesus answered questions asked by many in His audience, and we are still asking the same questions today.

His sermon turned sharply toward the end, moving from sharing information to application. What did Jesus want His audience to do? Should they simply feel content that they had the opportunity to listen to the most anointed, insightful, and wisest teacher ever? Or did Jesus expect the hearers to apply the content? Did His words necessitate action on their part? Let's see.

Matthew 7:24–29 (New King James Version [NKJV]) states:

> "Therefore, whoever hears these sayings of Mine, and does them, I will liken him to a wise man who built his house on the rock: and the rain descended, the floods came, and the winds blew and beat on that house; and it did not fall, for it was founded on the Rock. But everyone who hears these sayings of Mine, and does not do them, will be like a foolish man who built his house on the sand: and the rain descended, the floods came, and the winds blew and beat on that house; and it fell. And great was its fall." And so it was when Jesus had ended these sayings, that

the people were astonished at His teaching, for
He taught them as one having authority, and not
as the scribes.

Granted that parts of the Bible are mysterious—I get that;
I love that— but Jesus's illustrative language doesn't seem
challenging to understand here. Mark Twain said, "It ain't
those parts of the Bible that I can't understand that bother me;
it is the parts that I do understand."

Once Jesus finished the bulk of His sermon, He wrapped
up His message and metaphorically placed the ball in the
hearers' court. What would they do with what they had heard?
Even today, too many believe that the extent of obedience is
in hearing sermons, so they attend church weekly, hearing
sermon after sermon, only to leave the church unchanged. You
can routinely attend the same church, sit on the same pew, sing
the same songs, and remain unprepared for the storms in life.

In essence, Jesus reminded them of their responsibility.
He had been faithful to teach the truth. Now, would they be
faithful to apply it? In a genuine sense, their lives depended on
their response.

Often, we focus too much on outer beauty. When riding
by a house, we may admire the windows, doors, and shutters,
but a house's most vital part is what you cannot see. While not
visual, it is essential for the structure's endurance. It's called
the foundation.

Hearing the truth but not obeying it results in a weak
foundation for life. Jesus called it "sand," which inevitably
collapses under pressure. Just as you would never construct
your house on sand, how much more should you guard against
building your life on it? Ignoring the truth leaves you unprepared
and vulnerable. Hearing but not obeying the Word will prove

costly. James addressed this when writing, "But don't just listen to God's word. You must do what it says. Otherwise, you are only fooling yourselves" (James 1:22 New Living Translation [NLT]).

Jesus's closing illustration amplifies his focus by highlighting the similarity between two men: they each built a house. Each man had a place where he could sleep and eat. But both houses were not prepared. You may say, "Prepared for what?" Storms. A strong foundation does not exempt you from life's storms but will equip you to weather them.

Do you want to build a resilient life? Sure you do. Resilience is being able to withstand the howling winds and downpours of life. Pictures of the aftermath of hurricanes and tornados remind us of the power of these storms and the devastation they bring. Yet sometimes, a visual reveals a tree or home still standing amid the debris. Jesus says your life can be like that. No matter how hard the winds blow or how high the waters rise, you can still be standing after the storms pass. Your life can be, according to Jesus, windproof.

"How is that possible?" you may ask. Well, let's see what Jesus says. Again, granted, I know particular parts of the Bible are mysterious but not this illustration. Jesus reminds us that the only way to have a strong foundation is to hear and obey the truth.

Take a close look at His words:

> "Therefore, whoever hears these words of Mine, and does them, I will liken to a wise man who built his house on the rock:" (Matthew 7:24 NKJV)

> "But everyone who hears these sayings of Mine, and does not do them, will be like a foolish man

who built his house on the sand." (Matthew 7:26 NKJV)

Only one of them applied the truth. The takeaway: It's vital to listen to the truth. It's more important to apply it.

Position Yourself to Hear the Truth of God's Word

Hearing the truth is essential, and local churches should serve as the centers of truth in our communities. Without question, local church attendance is not even hit-and-miss, even for some who refer to themselves as church members. For far too many, church attendance has left town: trips to the lake/beach, sports events, and other venues for hobbies have made church optional at best. Some seem to spend all week putting their ox in the ditch to get him out each Sunday conveniently. I'm in no way against occasional getaways. I encourage them. But when church attendance becomes occasional, it usually indicates the presence of an idol. Too often, we occasionally do what we should consistently do.

In my ministry, I've heard, "I don't have to go to church to go to heaven." These critics, often pseudo-theologians, misunderstand my point. I'm not talking about going to heaven. I'm talking about how to build a strong foundation in life. This requires hearing the truth, obeying the truth, and living in fellowship with other believers. Again, to windproof your life, you must listen to the truth. And God has established the local church to serve as a truth center in our lives. Look at Paul's words: "but if I am delayed, *I write* so that you may know how you ought to conduct yourself in the house of God, which is the church of the living God, the pillar and ground of the truth" (1 Timothy 3:15 NKJV).

Paul also wrote, "So then faith *comes* by hearing, and hearing by the word of God" (Romans 10:17 NKJV).

Jesus was a Master Teacher. He had the perfect blend of content and power, and teaching was one of His gifts to the church. Specifically, Paul refers to this gift in Ephesians 4:11 and Romans 12:7:

> And He Himself gave some *to be* apostles, some prophets, some evangelists, and some pastors and teachers, for the equipping of the saints for the work of the ministry, for the edification of the body of Christ, till we all come to the unity of the faith and of the knowledge of the Son of God, to a perfect man, to the measure of the stature of the fullness of Christ. (Ephesians 4:11 NKJV)

> Having then gifts differing according to the grace that is given to us, let us use them: if prophecy, let us prophesy in proportion to our faith; or ministry, let us use it in our ministering; he who teaches, in teaching. (Romans 12:6–7 NKJV)

Personal Bible study is essential, but learning from gifted Bible teachers and preachers is also valuable. Jesus uniquely equips some to prepare and share the truth of God's Word. As a pastor/teacher, I value listening to other teachers. There are a few whom God has used more than others to bring conviction, course correction, and encouragement to me personally.

The unique blend of ignorance and pride often leads people to conclude they don't need any connection to a local church. Such nonsense is indeed not found in the New Testament. Believers, when possible, should be committed to a local church for many reasons, not the least of which is being under the anointed teaching/preaching of the Word.

Paul, writing to Timothy, a pastor, stated, "I charge *you* therefore before God and the Lord Jesus Christ, who will judge the living and the dead at His appearing and His kingdom: Preach the word! Be ready in season *and* out of season. Convince, rebuke, exhort, with all longsuffering and teaching" (2 Timothy 4:1–2 NKJV).

I will never forget an experience years ago concerning the power of hearing the Bible preached. A fellow pastor and I had what is, where I'm from, commonly referred to as a falling out. That's a South Georgia way of saying we had an argument that led to a break in friendship. As a side note, I do not recall what initiated the conflict.

I knew things had to change. I attended an annual Bible conference at a local church near my hometown, and the Lord was waiting for me there. During the sermon, I felt convicted and received clear instructions from the Word and the Spirit to seek restoration with my *former* friend. So I set up an appointment and entered his office, and he welcomed me, literally, with open arms. Although we briefly discussed the issue, his gesture said everything that needed to be said, and restoration was immediate. To this day, he is a good friend and someone I genuinely love. Restoration happened because I heard the Word preached, and I thankfully obeyed.

Let's focus on the main point of this introduction to *Windproof.* We must hear and apply the Word to windproof our lives. I listened to the preacher's words at the conference that day, but the question remained: would I obey? Obedience to the Word strengthened my faith and walk with the Lord. Only listening to the Word and not obeying it would have weakened me spiritually, not to mention ruining a once cherished friendship. The strength we long for and need comes from obedience—the application of truth.

Perhaps you remember Merthiolate. Years ago, this concoction was the bane of many boys and girls. Just the sight of it was enough to terrorize. But it no doubt decreased the spread of infection. On the Merthiolate bottle were instructions concerning its application. As long as the Merthiolate was in the bottle, it could not help. The application was essential. You no doubt get the point. Jesus, at the end of the Sermon on the Mount, reminds the hearers that application is necessary.

Windproof focuses on applying the truth, encouraging you to move from intention to action. I heard John Maxwell say, "Most Christians are educated well beyond their level of obedience." That stuck. I hope the following thoughts and words help build a firm foundation in your life. As you read every page, plan to apply truth as the Holy Spirit speaks to you. No matter what storm you face, your life can be *windproof.*

What will you do with the truth you hear?

1

WHERE IT ALL BEGINS

He was smart. Probably rich. Certainly powerful. Nicodemus was the man on the receiving end of the most memorable verse in the Bible: John 3:16. Vain religion had left him empty and curious, and curiosity led him into an enlightening conversation with Jesus.

That conversation with Nicodemus stemmed from Jesus saying, "Most assuredly, I say to you, unless one is born again, he cannot see the kingdom of God" (John 3:3 NKJV).

Nicodemus's response revealed his curiosity: "How can a man be born when he is old? Can he enter a second time into his mother's womb and be born?" (John 3:4 NKJV).

The birth of a child is an unrivaled earthly experience. Even the most stoic men seldom hold back emotion as a baby makes its miraculous entrance. Every move and sound of the baby is giggled over with delight. Joy, hope, and optimism fill the room, as they should. Birth creates a sense of wonder. For many, the birth of a child leads to the worship of the Giver of life.

Practically speaking, birth is the experience we have all had that marks the beginning. Granted, without question, life begins at conception. Still, we celebrate birthdays each year to remember the day of our birth into the world.

You can probably anticipate the direction of this conversation. Jesus's words to Nicodemus were unique. It's safe to conclude from Nicodemus's reaction that he had never heard the truth as he heard it from Jesus. *Born again?* What could that possibly mean?

As is often the case, Nicodemus attempted to process spiritual language with an unspiritual mind. This misreading led him to ask a question that, when closely considered, is ridiculous. The image of reentering your mother's womb—give that one some thought. I digress.

But Jesus meant what He said. Even if Nicodemus could not immediately understand it, it was no less true. Jesus doubled down. He said, "Most assuredly, I say to you, unless one is born of water and the Spirit, he cannot enter the kingdom of God. That which is born of the flesh is flesh, and that which is born of the Spirit is spirit. Do not marvel that I said to you, 'You must be born again'" (John 3:5–7 NKJV).

The second birth is more miraculous than the first. It's spiritual. Being born again is an experience that happens in the life of a person who, of course, has been born physically. Jesus spoke to Nicodemus about a necessary experience with God everyone needs but not everyone has. Like physical birth, the second birth marks a beginning.

This chapter is foundational, as implied by its title. The principles outlined in the rest of the book will make sense only to those who are born again. The born-again experience lays the groundwork for understanding spiritual truths. "But the natural man does not receive the things of the Spirit of God, for they are foolishness to him; nor can he know *them*, because they are spiritually discerned" (1 Corinthians 2:14 NKJV).

One of my heroes in the faith is a man named Doug Heard. You will become more familiar with him as you finish this book. Doug's name is not known to most readers. He never wrote a book or a song and was not a preacher. After becoming a Christian late in life, he followed Jesus until he went home to be with the Lord. While he was not famous, I believe the devil knew his name due to his unwavering devotion to Jesus and his powerful testimony.

When I became the pastor of TruthPoint, Doug began attending. We were strangers at the time. Initially, virtually all were strangers to me at the little church in Lakeland, Georgia. I was excited to be there, and the excitement remains after twenty-seven years.

I noticed Doug was emotional as he departed the church. He did not appear to me as a man who cried quickly, but the tears rolling down his face told a story I would soon learn. One day, Doug visited me at the pastorium where I lived. He pulled up and parked in my front yard with a massive bulldog rising above the bed of his pickup. I would later learn to love that dog.

I have a clear memory of that day; in a way, it feels like it happened just yesterday. Doug was known as one of the toughest men in the county. I was raised in South Georgia around many tough people, and I could tell Doug was a man's man. As he pulled into my yard with his impressive bulldog, and given his reputation, I could not help but wonder if my ministry, or my life, was about to end abruptly.

It did mark the end but not for me. This occasion marked an end for Doug. A short conversation made it clear that God was at work in Doug's heart. He was being brought to the second birth. Despite being well into his sixties, that day, he became a babe in Christ.

We found ourselves in his living room, discussing spiritual matters. In that way, that conversation between Doug and me was like Jesus's conversation with Nicodemus. Doug was infected with the love of Christ and was never cured. God covered him with grace, and it showed and showed and showed.

Fast-forward to Doug's deathbed. I cried as I drove to his house. I walked into the same living room where he had been born again not so many years before. The first place I saw him come alive spiritually served as the setting where I would see him for the last time alive physically on earth. There was a touch of sad but hopeful irony there.

I will never forget him taking his enormous, strong hand and reaching for mine. He looked at me as if to say, "It's OK. I'm at peace. Don't worry." That experience marked me. Doug was different. I never knew the barroom brawler nor witnessed the many stories told. Instead, I knew him after his born-again experience. I watched him grow into a man of tremendous grace, tenderness, and wisdom. I could water a ten-acre South Georgia cotton field with the tears I saw him cry at the name of Jesus. The born-again experience marked an end and a beginning for Doug. That was the starting line for the race God had set before him. He ran it well.

Being born again is foundational, much like physical birth. All life experiences can only occur because you were born; the second birth functions similarly. The promises of God are for those who have been born again. The Spirit of God is given to those who have experienced the second birth. Those born again are adopted into the family of God. They are joint heirs with Jesus Christ.

Consider Saul of Tarsus. He ultimately penned numerous books in the New Testament but only after his born-again experience. Before his conversion, with legal documents in his hand and hatred in his heart, he headed for Damascus. Acts 9:1–2 (NKJV) states, "Then Saul, still breathing threats and murder against the disciples of the Lord, went to the high priest and asked letters from him to the synagogues of Damascus, so that if he found any who were of the Way, whether men or women, he might bring them bound to Jerusalem."

To say that Saul hated those of the Way (Christians) is no overstatement. He had already consented to the death of Stephen. So he felt justified, with legal rights, to severely persecute those who found hope in the Nazarene. But one experience would radically change Saul's heart and, thus, his plans. Here's a short description of what happened: "As he journeyed he came near Damascus, and suddenly a light shone around him from heaven. Then he fell to the ground, and heard a voice saying to him, 'Saul, Saul, why are you persecuting Me?'" (Acts 9:3–4 NKJV).

This experience changed Saul from the inside out. He was born again. He later wrote, "Therefore, if anyone *is* in Christ, *he is* a new creation; old things have passed away; behold, all things have become new" (2 Corinthians 5:17 NKJV).

Back to Doug. I will never forget him telling me not long after being born again, "Jesus Christ changed my want-tos." At that time, Doug simply articulated, in his way, the truth in

2 Corinthians 5:17. I will share more about this part of Doug's story in chapter 7.

Now, back to Saul of Tarsus. He was changed. He went from desiring to kill Christians to having a holy determination to convert everyone to Christ. He had been, well, born again. And that experience brought about an internal change that led to changed actions. That's the way it works. That's what happens with the new birth.

Being born again is an internal, spiritual experience. This truth is what stumped Nicodemus. He tried to figure out how someone could reenter his mother's womb and exit again, signifying a second birth. He could not understand the spiritual language of Jesus.

The topic of being born again is intentionally placed at the beginning of this book. The rest of the chapters have no particular order, but this first chapter does. Why? Because being born again is foundational. It's where the race begins.

Marriages have been saved because a husband, wife, or both were born again. Alcoholics have finally found the strength to break their addiction because of being born again. Some intoxicated by materialism have found contentment due to the second birth. Many who have stared into the dark eyes of hopelessness and depression have found the hope they longed for through the second birth. There is no chance of having a windproof life apart from being born again. No chance! One more time. No chance!

The testimonies are too numerous to count. Millions upon millions have found power and peace because of being born again. Since the day Jesus taught this concept to Nicodemus, many have experienced it. From every corner of the earth, people have spiritually gone from rags to riches through their second birth.

Annually, millions of dollars are paid by people searching for ways to improve their lives. But most of this is material in nature. How can I look better? How can I make more money? How can I climb the corporate ladder? How can I? How can I? How can I? But nothing positions a person for the abundant life (John 10:10) like being born again. No amount of money, beauty, popularity, or power can lead to an abundant life, not the kind Jesus gives. Indeed, the world's vain qualities can offer temporary satisfaction and short-term pleasure, but they have no power to prosper spiritually; only God can do that.

One more story. Many years ago, after graduating from high school, I tried my hand at the world of construction. I had never been interested in constructing buildings, which soon became evident. I was quickly relegated to being the lumber carrier. I'm sure that's not the proper term, but it works.

Each morning, I would get in a van for forty-five minutes en route to the job site. Some mornings, I was accompanied by two men. On occasion, rather than beginning the day with eggs and toast, they smoked marijuana. It was a wild ride!

I was eventually fired from that job. I liked the men, and I think they liked me. I was not lazy. I worked diligently. That wasn't the problem. The problem was I knew more about brain surgery than I did construction. I was a liability. So I was fired, though the boss was very nice about it. I understood.

This story is interesting because of what happened many years later. After being away at Liberty University, I returned to my small hometown. One afternoon, I pulled into the parking lot of the local grocery store. In front of my vehicle was a church van. That's not particularly interesting, but the man driving got my attention.

One of my buddies from the back of the old construction van was at the wheel. I like to say my first thought was, "He has stolen the church van!" That would not have necessarily been a judgmental thought. It would have been very understandable. You must remember my previous experiences with him in a van.

As I approached him, I noticed something different. The look on his face, in his eyes, was not what I had witnessed in the construction van. Instead, he had something drugs never gave him. He had joy. He beamed with hope.

He began to tell me how his life had changed and that he now drove the church van to pick up kids for church. He said, without using these exact words, "Since you saw me last, I've been born again." The dead man I had known years before was alive. In Christ, he found the peace and joy drugs had promised but never delivered.

Consider the rest of this book as the framing and finishing of a home. But consider *this* chapter the foundation. First, "you must be born again" (John 3:7).

Windproof Challenge:

You may be reading this, and God is speaking to your heart about being born again. Remember, Nicodemus was religious but empty. He was lost. Doug was not religious, but like Nicodemus, he was empty. So what did these men have in common? Each needed to be born again.

Remember, knowing you should repent and give your life to Christ is insufficient. You must respond to God's amazing grace and the drawing of His Spirit. Repent. And call on the name of the Lord to save you. You can do that now. Look at this prayer. If God is speaking to you, respond from your heart and with your mouth (Romans 10:9):

> Dear God, today, I know I need to be born
> again. I believe Jesus came into this world and
> died on the cross for my sins. I believe He was

resurrected three days later. I repent of my sin and turn to you. Thank you for saving me. Please fill me with Your Spirit and use me for Your glory. In Jesus's name. Amen.

2

PRAYER

The disciples of Jesus knew, as do we, the necessity of prayer for those who desire to live a godly, windproof life. Though prayer is likely the most neglected privilege in the average Christian's life, we instinctively know we should spend time communicating with the Lord. And without question, prayer is essential to placing our lives on firm footing. After observing the prayer life of Jesus, the disciples requested insight concerning prayer. Luke 11:1 (NKJV) states, "Now it came to pass, as He was praying in a certain place, when He ceased, *that* one of His disciples said to Him, 'Lord, teach us to pray, as John also taught his disciples.'"

Though, or perhaps because Jesus was the Son of God, He prayed not occasionally but often. As the Son of Man, He demonstrated for all sons of men the necessity of withdrawing for focused time with the Father. "So He Himself *often* withdrew into the wilderness and prayed" (Luke 5:16 NKJV).

Why withdraw? What was the purpose of leaving the thronging crowds? After all, isn't the masses what most preachers desire? Why leave those He was there to touch? We should learn from Jesus's discipline. To effectively touch people with the power of God, we must purposely withdraw from them to focus on the Father.

Prayer is a gift. God did not have to make Himself available to people. As deists wrongfully conclude, He could have created the world, spun it into motion, and then exited the stage without intending to interact with His creation. But that's not the case, not even close.

God did not withdraw from His creation. Instead, He came to us (more on this later in the chapter). Story after story in Old Testament scripture reveals God's interaction and open ear to the Jewish people. And although the New Covenant is better than the Old (Hebrews 8:6), even the Old Covenant offered access to God for qualified Jews. So let's consider a few stories from the Old Testament.

Consider King Jehoshaphat. As king of Judah, he faced an overwhelming challenge.

> It happened after this *that* the people of Moab with the people of Ammon, and *others* with them besides the Ammonites, came to battle against Jehoshaphat. Then some came and told Jehoshaphat, saying, "A great multitude is coming against you from beyond the sea, from

Syria; and they are in Hazazon Tamar" (which is En Gedi). And Jehoshaphat feared, and set himself to seek the Lord, and proclaimed a fast throughout all Judah. (2 Chronicles 20:1–3 NKJV)

You probably haven't received news of a national army alliance coming against you, but you've likely experienced the same fear as Jehoshaphat. Sometimes, an onslaught of bills comes, your job is threatened, or a child goes astray. These occasions, along with others, have the potential to strike your heart with one of—if not the greatest of our enemies—fear.

In the face of an overwhelming challenge, Jehoshaphat prayed. Prayer was his first option, not his last resort. And his prayer saved thousands of lives. After Jehoshaphat prayed, a prophet, Jahaziel, sent this message: "You will not *need* to fight this *battle*. Position yourselves, stand still and see the salvation of the Lord, who is with you, O Judah and Jerusalem! Do not fear or be dismayed; tomorrow go out against them, for the Lord is with you" (2 Chronicles 20:17 NKJV).

They saw salvation with the Lord. And so can you.

We have all had difficult days. It's part of living in a sinful, fallen world. But imagine being Hezekiah. After Hezekiah had suffered from sickness for some time, Isaiah, a major prophet, came to his house with a simple message, "Set your house in order, for you shall die, and not live" (2 Kings 20:1 NKJV).

The warning was devastating. And the bearer of the news was Isaiah, one of the most reputable prophets in scripture. So should Hezekiah just accept that this news was unchangeable, or should he pray? Well, he chose the latter. The Bible says, "Then he turned his face toward the wall, and prayed to the Lord, saying, 'Remember now, O Lord, I pray, how I have walked before you in truth and with a loyal heart, and have done *what was* good in Your sight.' And Hezekiah wept bitterly" (2 Kings 20:2–3 NKJV).

This is an Old Covenant prayer and sounds like it, but God saw his heart, heard his prayer, and answered. Look at God's response. "And it happened, before Isaiah had gone into the middle court, that the word of the Lord came to him, saying, 'Return and tell Hezekiah the leader of My people, "Thus says the Lord, the God of David your father. I have heard your prayer, I have seen your tears; surely I will heal you. On the third day you shall go up to the house of the Lord"'" (2 Kings 20:4–5 NKJV).

The original message from Isaiah could have taken away Hezekiah's will to pray. He could have concluded, as some do, that praying was useless. He could have thought, "At this point, this is just how it is. What will be, will be," or one of the latest clichés, "It is what it is." I like to say, "It is what it is. But it ain't what it's going to be." Unfortunately, fatalism has flooded the church and quenched the flames of fervent prayer. Fatalistic theology has crept into the church primarily through the halls of academia and has robbed many of an effective prayer life. If what will be, will be, why pray? It's that simple. Those who teach and believe this fatalism have carefully crafted responses to criticism like this. But in the end, they are virtually prayerless and lead others to prayerlessness. It's sad. Through faithful prayer, though, Hezekiah believed that God changed things and lived because he believed that.

Let's consider one last Old Covenant example: Elijah. A New Covenant writer highlighted Elijah's prayer life. James, using Elijah as an example, wrote:

Confess *your* trespasses to one another, and pray for one another, that you may be healed. The effective, fervent prayer of a righteous man avails much. Elijah was a man with a nature like ours, and he prayed earnestly that it would not rain; and it did not rain on the land for three years and six months. And he prayed again, and the heaven gave rain, and the earth produced its fruit. (James 5:16–18 NKJV)

Notice James reminds the reader that Elijah "was a man with a nature like ours." Why did he say that? I suspect because he knew believers would conclude Elijah was a superbeliever with access to God unavailable to common believers. James wanted to ensure we understood we could pray and have similar results as Elijah. His effectual, fervent prayer life delivered results that benefited many people and glorified God. And James wanted all believers to know that ours can too.

Fast-forward. The Old Covenant closes and there are, in essence, four hundred years of silence from heaven. Eventually, a new prophet arrived as the forerunner of the promised Messiah. John the Baptist fulfilled his ultimate purpose. "The next day John saw Jesus coming toward him, and said, 'Behold the Lamb of God who takes away the sin of the world!'" (John 1:29 NKJV).

Of course, John spoke of Jesus's future work on the cross. His death on the cross was sufficient to save the world. In 1 John, the Bible states, "And He Himself is the propitiation for our sins, and not for ours only but also for the whole world" (1 John 2:2 NKJV).

I like the way the New Living Translation (NLT) states this: "He Himself is the sacrifice that atones for our sins—and not only our sins but the sins of all the world" (1 John 2:2 NLT).

The atonement is not limited as some teach. Instead, Jesus's atoning work is sufficient to save everyone on this sin-stricken planet but only applies to those who trust Him. Some will perform hermeneutical gymnastics to get around this truth, but the simplicity of this verse rises above any confusing (often referred to as deep) interpretation. Of course, the great truths of the cross cannot be sufficiently expounded upon in any book. However, I would like to consider one aspect of the cross pertaining to prayer: access. The forgiveness of sin was essential to access God, so God made provision through the death of Jesus at Calvary.

The use of object lessons is a powerful form of communication. The Bible presents a wide array of these expressions of truth. For example, the valley of dry bones was an object lesson demonstrating the Spirit and the Word's power to bring restoration and revival (Ezekiel 37:1–14). Jesus and the woman at the well were object lessons on how Jesus is an internal well bringing constant refreshing to parched souls (John 4:1–38). In Galatians 4, Paul used Sarai (the free woman) and Hagar (the bondwoman) to portray the vast difference between the Old and New Covenants. These are small samples of object lessons in the Bible.

My favorite object lesson in the Bible happened on the day Jesus died on the cross. When Jesus took his last breath, the earth quaked, graves opened, and many Old Testament saints were resurrected (Matthew 27:51–52). There was another phenomenon replete with symbolism that occurred. The temple's veil was torn from top to bottom, which, in my opinion, was the object lesson of all object lessons: "Then, behold, the veil of the temple was torn in two from top to bottom; and the earth quaked, and the rocks were split, and the graves were opened; and many bodies of the saints who had fallen asleep were raised" (Matthew 27:51–52 NKJV).

Matthew, Mark, and Luke each document the tearing of the veil. Luke also reveals that the sun ceased shining when the Son stopped breathing.

Amazingly, though, the temple had a response of its own. The death of the Nazarene deeply impacted the core of religious experience for Jews. I would argue there could not have been a more significant change at the temple. The veil was a barrier, a stopping point for all humanity except for the high priest, and he could walk through it only once a year.

The Holy of Holies was small but undoubtedly the most significant space on earth. It housed the law of God (Ten Commandments), a jar of manna, and Aaron's rod. That is not all though. These objects were inside the Ark of the Covenant, which claimed space in this sacred cube. Most significantly, the presence of God was there.

Please do not imagine the torn veil resembling the curtains in your bedroom window. Instead, this curtain was inches thick and hung in the innermost part of the temple. The curtain shouted separation. On the Day of Atonement, one man, the high priest, could go beyond it. With blood in hand, he would go in and, most likely trembling, sprinkle blood on the mercy seat on behalf of the people for forgiveness. It has been widely taught that a rope was tied around the ankle of the high priest in case he died while performing his duties. If anyone else dared go beyond the veil, even if it were to retrieve the dead body of the high priest, certain death would occur. Talk about forbidden ground! Access was denied if you were not the high priest on that day of the year. That is until Jesus died on the cross.

The Hebrew writer makes a startling remark concerning the believer's access to the throne room of God. He writes, "And so, dear brothers and sisters, we can boldly enter heaven's Most Holy Place because of the blood of Jesus" (Hebrews 10:19 NLT).

This is another reason the Gospel message was so offensive to many religious Jews. To them, the high priest of Israel had special access to God. Now, through Jesus, believers claimed that the blood shed by a carpenter's son had torn the veil, making it possible for anyone to enter in the name of Jesus. This is described as the priesthood of believers. No earthly priest is needed. Our High Priest, Jesus, is sufficient.

Now, consider all God did to make it possible for us to pray. The most common of all men and women are invited to communicate with God without a human mediator, another reason we call it good news.

Are you taking advantage of this privilege? Most of us would leap at the opportunity if invited to the Oval Office. However, we are invited to a much more prestigious place than that. The very throne room of God is accessible. In Hebrews 4:16 (NLT), the writer states, "So let us come boldly to the throne of our gracious God. There we will receive His mercy, and we will find grace to help us when we need it most."

The veil is torn. The invitation is open. Will you come?

As mentioned previously, prayer was a significant part of the earthly life of Jesus. His continual retreat to the mountain apparently caught the attention of the disciples. In a separate text, Jesus warned His listeners:

> "When you pray, don't be like the hypocrites
> who love to pray publicly on street corners
> and in the synagogues where everyone can

see them. I tell you the truth, that is all the
reward they will ever get. But when you pray,
go away by yourself, shut the door behind you,
and pray to your Father in private. Then your
Father, who sees everything, will reward you.
When you pray, don't babble on and on like
the Gentiles do. They think their prayers are
answered merely by repeating their words again
and again." (Matthew 6:5–7 NLT)

Here, Jesus reminds us that motive matters when it comes
to prayer. Effective prayer is not a formal religious exercise
dominated by empty, repeated words. James, Jesus's half-
brother, scolded the readers of his letter concerning prayer. He
wrote, "You ask and do not receive, because you ask amiss, that
you may spend it on your pleasures" (James 4:3 NKJV).

According to Jesus and James, effective prayer derives from
sincerity and humility.

In 2015, I was diagnosed with a brain tumor. The pathology
report later determined it was not malignant. The problem,
though, was that it was the size of a peach, near the stem of
my brain, and already causing noticeable symptoms. I will never
forget seeing the image following my MRI. I was devastated.
I was the daddy to three beautiful girls and husband to an
amazing wife. The thought of leaving them seemed more than
my heart could bear.

I can't remember an atheist or agnostic reaching out to me
during this time. After all, what do they have to say at such a
devastating time? But countless followers of Christ contacted
Jenn and me to let us know they were praying for us. First
Baptist Church in Homerville, GA, where I surrendered to
Christ, hosted a large prayer service, and anointed me with oil.

Not long before the day of my surgery, Jenn and I attended New Prospect Community Church, and fervent prayer was offered at the altar. On another occasion, two men slid into my bedroom in the dark of night, quietly prayed for me, and then slipped out.

God spared my life. I will never forget my surgeon's words at my first follow-up appointment. He said, "The Grim Reaper came for you. It just wasn't your time." This experienced and reputable surgeon revealed that death knocked on my door. What happened? I will forever believe it was the faithful prayers of God's people. But fatalists conclude, "That's just how things were supposed to be." I don't believe that for a second. Instead, I know people of God boldly accessed the throne of grace because of the blood shed by Jesus, and God healed my body. I know this may create questions concerning some who have not been healed, but I firmly believe God moved a mountain out of my life due to faithful prayer.

Many who read this have sat through numerous sermons on prayer. Unfortunately, you may have left some of these sermons feeling condemned for not praying more. Granted, we should be convicted by the Holy Spirit for prayerlessness. A lack of prayer on behalf of a Christian may be rooted in laziness, busyness, pride, or, as previously mentioned, fatalistic theology. No reason or excuse for prayerlessness is acceptable.

Some feel the need to fix what Jesus said. These people often leave no room for God to work outside their tight, well-wrapped theological box. Consequently, they seldom, if ever, see Him work beyond the confines of their rigid theology. Take, for instance, what Jesus said concerning prayer in Mark 11:23–26 (NKJV):

> "For assuredly, I say to you, whoever says to this mountain, 'Be removed and be cast into

the sea,' and does not doubt in his heart, but believes that those things he says will be done, he will have whatever he says. Therefore I say to you, whatever things you ask when you pray, believe that you receive *them,* and you will have *them.* And whenever you stand praying, if you have anything against anyone, forgive him, that your Father in heaven may also forgive you your trespasses. But if you do not forgive, neither will your Father in heaven forgive your trespasses."

Taken in context, Jesus mentions two significant obstacles to mountain-moving prayer: doubt and unforgiveness. These double assassins will limit, if not eliminate, the power in your prayer life. Think about it. Jesus says the mountains in your life can be cast into the sea. He uses metaphorical language. Still, Jesus means what He says. The impossible is possible through prayer unhindered by doubt and bitterness.

I will not attempt to cover these topics now because I will deal with faith and forgiveness in the coming chapters. Nevertheless, hear Jesus. If you harbor doubt and cling to unforgiveness, just know one or both can keep those mountains out of the sea and in your life. This truth must be what the psalmist was communicating when writing, "If I had not confessed the sin in my heart, the Lord would not have listened" (Psalm 66:18 NLT).

The mountain Jesus speaks about is anything in our lives that only God can handle. David's mountain was named Goliath. One of Moses's mountains was the Red Sea. Joshua's mountain was the Jericho wall. And let's not forget that our Savior faced a mountain—the tomb. And it was no match for His power.

What is the name of your mountain? What are you facing now that is too big or overwhelming to defeat? Jesus gave His promise concerning prayer because He knew we would face mountains. What must we do? Pray. It's that simple. What we needed more than anything to see the mountains of this life hurled into the sea was access to God, which God gave us through Christ.

Is this chapter prompting you to pray on behalf of a friend or family member? If so, don't hesitate. Pray. Do you need to pray a prayer of surrender to the Lord? If you do, He waits and welcomes those who come to Him, waving the white flag of surrender. Or maybe you simply need to offer the Lord a prayer of gratitude. If you're a parent, you know the feeling you get when your child thanks you without any follow-up requests. Of course, God loves to hear your appeals, but prayers of exclusive gratitude are special.

Everyone desires peace. When I speak, I often say, "I don't know everyone here today, but I know what everyone wants—peace." And you know what? I have never had anyone interrupt, saying, "Nope. Not me!" Everyone wants peace, but not everyone has it. Everyone born again has access to peace and contentment because they have access to the God of all comfort (2 Corinthians 1:3). Consider Paul's words to the Philippian believers:

> Don't worry about anything; instead, pray about everything. Tell God what you need, and thank Him for all He has done. Then you will experience God's peace, which exceeds anything we can understand. His peace will guard your hearts and minds as you live in Christ Jesus. (Philippians 4:6–7 NLT)

Paul reveals another reason to develop a prayerful life. Peace is at stake. We forfeit peace because we neglect prayer. By inspiration of the Holy Spirit, Paul ties peace to prayer, and we can't untie it. These two are joined as closely as faith is to works (James 2:17) and love is to unity (Colossians 3:14). Simply put: no prayer, no peace.

So much of Paul's writings in scripture are informative. With wisdom from God and inspiration from the Holy Spirit, the humble theologian shared insights concerning the Gospel that had been downloaded to him by Jesus (Galatians 1:11–12). But he made a simple request to his brothers and sisters in First and Second Thessalonians. He simply said, "Brethren, pray for us" (1 Thessalonians 5:25 NKJV).

In 2 Thessalonians, Paul took this call for prayer a little further. He wrote, "Finally, brethren, pray for us, that the word of the Lord may run *swiftly* and be glorified, just as it was with you, and that we may be delivered from unreasonable and wicked men; for not all have faith" (2 Thessalonians 3:1–2 NKJV).

This fearless, passionate propagator of the Gospel not only prayed but coveted the church's prayers. He knew the success of his enormous task was largely dependent on prayer, from him and others on his behalf.

Paul requested the church in Thessalonica to pray for his ministry and efforts to spread the Gospel. Knowing some people would oppose his vision to share Christ with the world, he sought the church's prayers. Why? Because he believed God would intervene in the work of the ministry. If Paul, this choice apostle, needed prayer, we do too!

The prayerlessness of many churches today is partly rooted in a sense of self-sufficiency. Technology, flashy stages, and talented people can be a recipe for disaster regarding the church's true mission. I do not conclude that those with these ingredients do not pray. But I certainly will not shy away from believing that many churches are fulfilling their artificial, man-centered mission without the need to pray. Prayer is not necessary if a church desires to draw and entertain people. Now, I know some will read this and conclude that I'm a stick-in-the-mud preacher who is against everything new. That's simply not true. It just seems that some do not need God to fulfill their shallow desires. But if a church sees hearts converted, marriages restored, bodies healed, and disciples made, somebody's praying whether they have a flashy stage or no stage at all. If my assessment doesn't pertain to you, don't be offended. If it does, I hope it offends you enough to get a vision from God that cannot be accomplished without prayer.

What do you believe God desires to accomplish in your life? I know that is a broad question. But I think a specific answer applies to all believers: fruit. The fruit of the Spirit is mentioned in Galatians 5:22–23 (NKJV): "But the fruit of the Spirit is love, joy, peace, longsuffering, kindness, goodness, faithfulness, gentleness, self-control. Against such there is no law."

Stay tuned. I'm going somewhere with this.

Then there's Jesus's teaching in Mark 4. He concludes that those with good ground for the seed of the Word bear much fruit: "But these are the ones sown on the good ground, those who hear the Word, accept *it,* and bear fruit: some thirtyfold, some sixty, and some a hundred" (Mark 4:20 NKJV).

Finally, there's John 15. This chapter of scripture has changed the lives of many who have trusted Christ as Savior but ceased looking to Him as their source for abundant life (John 10:10). Jesus, using the connection between a vine and branch, reminds the reader of who is the vine (Jesus) and who is the branch (us). So many of the issues we have in life derive from an identity crisis resulting from our struggle to be the vine. In one verse of that flawless chapter, Jesus reminds us that a believer must abide in the vine—Christ—to bear fruit. And though there may be several ways to abide, continual prayer is undoubtedly central. Perhaps this is what Paul had in mind when writing, "Pray without ceasing" (1 Thessalonians 5:17 NKJV).

Jesus said, "I am the vine, you are the branches. He who abides in Me, and I in him, bears much fruit; for without Me you can do nothing" (John 15:5 NKJV).

To abide in Christ denotes constant communion. Again, this is not limited to prayer but certainly includes it. So prayer is essential if you want to windproof your life. This precept should encourage believers to pray. Do you want power for living? Learn to pray. Do you want peace amid the turbulent winds of this world? Of course, you do. Learn to pray. Do you want to live a fruitful life? I know you do. Later, in John 15, Jesus reminded His listeners, "These things I have spoken to you, that My joy may remain in you, and that your joy may be full" (John 15:11 NKJV).

We should not be surprised that the disciples asked Jesus to teach them how to pray. They knew that victory in this life was connected to prayer. They knew prayer was more than well-rehearsed words carelessly lofted before a meal or sporting event. They understood something extraordinary happened when Jesus retreated to the mountain, intentionally leaving people who needed Him. His discipline to seek time and location away from people to be with the Father, at least in part, led to their request for teaching concerning prayer. Later, after their request, Jesus went to the cross and laid down His life. Indeed, His death provided atonement—sufficient payment for sin that had brought separation. But it offered even more. The veil was torn.

Access to God was then available so that all who would come to God through Christ could see mountains cast into the sea, and amid the swirling winds of life, they could remain windproof.

Windproof Challenge:

It's one thing to know you should pray. It's another to pray. Remember, those whose lives are windproof not only know they should pray, but they pray. Do you need to begin today? You can.

There are books galore about prayer. Many of them are very helpful and encouraging. I recommend reading biographies of prayer warriors. They are easy to find. But even if you read every word of every book written on prayer, it will not windproof your life. The strength and stability you need will not come from reading books on prayer but from praying. Today is the day to begin. Why wait any longer to enjoy access to God, whose Son, with His blood, paved the way so you could come boldly to the throne of grace and find all the help you ever need?

3

GENEROSITY

To truly enjoy the things money can buy, you must first possess the qualities money can't buy. For your life to be windproof, you must have a biblical approach to money and possessions. The love of money and the stuff it can purchase lead to instability. Those who build their lives on the sinking sand of materialism too often live in misery, surrounded by many things that promise happiness but don't deliver because they can't deliver what they've promised. Money can buy you a fine bed but not a good night's sleep. Money can buy you a beautiful house but not a blessed marriage. Money can pay your tuition at a prestigious university but not give you the wisdom of God.

These facts and many more do not stop people from pursuing money at the expense of relationships with spouses, children, and, most sadly, God. My words may have you thinking I believe money is evil. You are wrong if that is your conclusion. It takes money to live. It takes money to minister effectively. As a pastor, I ask people to give money regularly. It's not money but the love of it that leads to instability and emptiness.

Paul addressed this issue with clarity in his first letter to Timothy. Dealing with the topic of greed, he wrote, "Now godliness with contentment is great gain. For we brought nothing into *this* world, and it is certain we can carry nothing out. And having food and clothing, with these we shall be content" (1 Timothy 6:6–8 NKJV).

The concept of financial contentment is foreign to many people. It is estimated that John D. Rockefeller was worth 1 percent of the American economy. Owning 90 percent of the oil and gas business earned him unimaginable wealth. When asked how much was enough, he famously responded, "Just a little bit more."

Sadly, billionaires do not have a monopoly on discontentment. Advertisers have mastered communicating discontentment to those far from being extremely wealthy. The advertising industry often reminds us why we need a sleeker phone, a bigger home, or a shinier car. Companies spend millions in advertising to manufacture discontentment. And their return on investment is impressive.

The longing for bigger and better is the root cause of the love of money. It's not the money as much as it is those things money can buy and the attention it brings that grow greed in the heart. Paul reminded Timothy, "For the love of money is the root of all *kinds of* evil. And some people, craving money, have wandered from the true faith and pierced themselves with many sorrows" (1 Timothy 6:10 NLT).

I remember sharing Christ with someone many years ago. At the end of the conversation, I asked him why he would not give his life to Christ. He previously quoted me the passage of scripture that says, "For what will it profit a man if he gains the whole world, and loses his own soul?" (Mark 8:36 NJKV).

So I was curious, after quoting that scripture to me, why wouldn't he surrender his life to Christ? His answer stunned me then and, years later, still saddens me. He said, "Because it would cost me too much."

This experience has always caused me to think of the man in the Bible, commonly called the rich, young ruler. His encounter with Christ had a sad ending. The question the man asked Jesus was appropriate. Everyone should ask it. But Jesus used the man's question to expose the pride and greed in his heart. He asked Jesus, "Good Teacher, what must I do to inherit eternal life?" (Mark 10:17 NLT).

Jesus used his question to reveal the thick coat of greed draped over his heart. Mark 10:21 (NLT) states, "Looking at the man, Jesus felt genuine love for him. 'There is still one thing you haven't done,' He told him. 'Go and sell all your possessions and give the money to the poor, and you will have treasure in heaven. Then come, follow Me.'"

If you're looking for bland religious answers, you better not ask Jesus questions. The question from the rich and powerful young man was appropriate, but Jesus could see the real problem. The young man had a god that needed to be dealt with first. Unfortunately, his god was his possessions. He rejected Jesus's offer. Mark 10:22 (NLT) says, "At this the man's face fell, and he went away sad, for he had many possessions."

Simply, this man was not ready to follow Jesus. Of course, like many, he considered heaven a better prospect than hell. But if Christ asked to be number one in his life, that was too much. His possessions possessed him and, ultimately, cost him dearly.

Jesus used this as a lesson for the disciples. As they watched and listened to the entire episode in real time, Jesus knew this was an opportunity to plant truth into fertile soil.

> Jesus looked around and said to his disciples, "How hard it is for the rich to enter the Kingdom of God!" This amazed them. But Jesus said again, "Dear children, it is very hard to enter the Kingdom of God. In fact, it is easier for a camel to go through the eye of a needle than for a rich person to enter the Kingdom of God!" (Mark 10:23–25 NLT)

This truth is certainly worth examining. The rich man walked away with his life on the shifting sand of materialism. Unwilling to follow Jesus, he continued to be ruled by his master, money. It's been said, "Money makes a good servant but a terrible master." The Bible says the young man left sorrowful. Like so many, he knew his possessions lacked the power to bring peace and fulfillment. Still, he would not turn them loose. The rich man reminds us of a common saying, "The poorest man in the world is the man who has nothing but money." A man I love once texted me. He achieved financial success at an early age but also learned that while money can buy things, the essential things in life are not for sale. He texted me, "I was so broke not too long ago. All I had was money."

Could the rich man have come to Jesus? Most certainly. Jesus's use of hyperbole was not uncommon. There are disagreements concerning Jesus's exaggerated illustration of the camel and the eye of the needle; however, there should not be disagreement over what He was communicating. Jesus was simply stating that the lure of materialism was strong. The rich, young ruler had just demonstrated its hold on his heart. A rich person can come to Jesus. But many, too many, will choose to worship at the altar of stuff rather than God. Jesus's hyperbolic statement sparked a question from the disciples, and Jesus answered. "And they were greatly astonished, saying among themselves, 'Who then can be saved?' But Jesus looked at them and said, 'With men it is impossible, but not with God; for with God all things are possible'" (Mark 10:26–27 NKJV).

There is a remedy for the greed that sickens our hearts: generosity. The thought of selling his possessions and giving the proceeds to the poor was more than the young man could fathom. He was severely stricken with greed. Jesus loved him but discerned greed's stranglehold around his heart. He asked him to sell all and give to the poor. This command from Jesus revealed the true master of the young man's life. He wanted money more than he wanted Jesus. Remember the words of Jesus, "No one can serve two masters. For you will hate one and love the other; you will be devoted to one and despise the other. You cannot serve God and be enslaved to money" (Matthew 6:24 NLT). It's been said, "No one has two masters, but everyone has one." Who or what is your master?

It's undeniable. God is a giver. The most well-known verse of scripture in the Bible states, "For God so loved the world that He gave His one and only Son, that whoever believes in Him should not perish but have everlasting life" (John 3:16 NLT).

God gave. He gave extravagantly. He gave willingly. His generous gift was motivated by love. This truth is at the heart of the Gospel. It's true, "We are never more like God than when we give."

The first church was marked by generosity. They sold personal possessions to share with their brothers and sisters in Christ. Acts 2:44–45 (NKJV) states, "Now all who believed were together, and had all things in common, and sold their possessions and goods, and divided them among all, as anyone had need."

With the wind of the Holy Spirit freshly blowing from Pentecost, the first church sacrificed personal possessions to meet the needs of their brothers and sisters in Christ. Undoubtedly, their generosity was instrumental in the first church, touching many people with the Gospel. Some have concluded the early church practiced communism because they "had all things in common." That's an absurd conclusion. Communism threatens people with the sword of the government to give up their possessions. The early church did it willingly—a big difference.

I'm not sure anything is more repulsive than greed and a lack of generosity. Churches corporately, and Christians in particular, should drip with generosity. Greed is a poor witness for God, who gave His only Son and continues to give so much. Paul reminds us, "Let there be no sexual immorality, impurity, or greed among you. Such sins have no place among God's people" (Ephesians 5:3 NLT).

Many people are loaded with both money and misery. Yet the world constantly tempts us to believe money is the cure for misery and despair. How many millionaires must commit suicide or die miserable and lonely before we realize money and possessions do not give us a truly abundant life? We certainly should not glorify poverty as some do. But Jesus reminded us that possessions alone do not provide the abundant life He offers. "Then He said, 'Beware! Guard against every kind of greed. Life is not measured by how much you own'" (Luke 12:15 NLT).

One of the temptations that come with wealth is pride. For multiple reasons, many believe net worth determines self-worth. Paul warns against this. In one verse, 1 Timothy 6:17 (NKJV), Paul gives a command that, if obeyed, would bring stability to some who are building their lives on the ever-shifting sand of materialism. He wrote, "Command those who are rich in this present age not to be haughty, nor to trust in uncertain riches but in the living God, who gives us all things to enjoy."

First, Paul warned against allowing wealth to cause haughtiness. This command was given because Paul recognized the tendency of wealth to produce pride in the heart of the one who has it. But it doesn't have to. Instead, wealth could lead to humility; however, too often, those rich with money are drunk with pride.

For this reason, a person's blessing can become their curse. The writer of Proverbs recognized this tendency. Look closely at his words: "O God, I beg two favors from You; let me have them before I die. First, help me never tell a lie. Second, give me neither poverty nor riches! Give me just enough to satisfy my needs. For if I grow rich, I may deny You and say, 'Who is the Lord?' And if I am too poor, I may steal and thus insult God's holy name" (Proverbs 30:7–9 NLT).

The writer of these words knew of the temptation of the rich to become haughty. He said riches could cause him to say, "Who is the Lord?" Of course, you may conclude that would never happen if you were to become incredibly wealthy. But this will most likely happen to those who believe it could not.

Secondly, in 1 Timothy 6:17, Paul warns against trusting "uncertain riches." We are supposed to trust God, not money. I will never forget reading the story of a group of men who met at the Edgewater Hotel in Chicago in 1923. These men's combined wealth was estimated to be worth more than the US Treasury. Look at this synopsis:

- Arthur Cutten was the greatest wheat speculator of his time; he died in a foreign country, unable to pay his debts.
- Albert Fall was the Secretary of Interior under President Harding; he died broke after being pardoned from prison to die at home.
- Leon Fraser, president of the International Settlements, committed suicide.
- Howard Hopson, president of the largest gas company, was mentally ill.
- Ivan Kreuger, who headed up the world's greatest monopoly, committed suicide.
- Jesse Livermore, the greatest bear on Wall Street, committed suicide.
- Charles Schwab, the president of the largest independent steel company, went bankrupt and lived on borrowed money for the later years of his life.
- Richard Whitney, the New York Stock Exchange president, spent time in Sing Prison.

These men, and many more, offer sufficient evidence as to why Paul commanded us not to trust in riches.

Paul states that God has "given us all things to enjoy." Notice that the verse mentions "things" and "enjoy." According to Paul, God has blessed us with things to enjoy. But there is a difference between enjoying things and worshiping things. Sadly, some conclude that God does not want us to enjoy the gifts He gives us in this world. God is not the cosmic killjoy. I believe God takes great pleasure in His people joyfully and gratefully enjoying a fine meal, family vacation, or sporting event. While this is true, our greatest blessings are those things money can't buy. But you must do some high-level misinterpreting not to conclude that Paul means what he says in writing: God "gives us richly all things to enjoy," but remember, life's greatest blessings can't be bought.

But let's get back to the thesis of this chapter. Generosity is a key to the kingdom and a necessity to withstand the storms in life. You cannot windproof your life with greed. A life of generosity and contentment brings stability. Greedy people are unstable because they have anchored their lives to the *created* rather than the Creator. Look at the words from Acts 20:35 (NKJV): "I have shown you in every way, by laboring like this, that you must support the weak. And remember the words of the Lord Jesus, that He said, 'It is more blessed to give than to receive.'"

The generous life is blessed.

Consider Zacchaeus. Money drove this *wee little man* so much that he stole from fellow Jews to help fuel the Roman Empire financially. As a result, he was despised, and that's putting it mildly. His bank account was full, but his heart was wanting. So, knowing Jesus would pass his way, the hands that had stolen so much gripped a sycamore tree so he could climb and get a glimpse of Christ. But while Zacchaeus climbed the tree to see Jesus, God had him there so Jesus could call his name. "And when Jesus came to the place, He looked up and saw him, and said to him, 'Zacchaeus, make haste and come down, for today I must stay at your house'" (Luke 19:5 NKJV).

Greed (Zacchaeus) met generosity (Jesus). The religious Jews would not dare seek fellowship with the likes of Zacchaeus. The Bible records the reaction of those who witnessed Jesus's company with the chief tax collector: "But when they saw it, they all complained, saying, 'He has gone to be a guest with a man who is a sinner'" (Luke 19:7 NKJV). If I were preaching at this point, I would say, "And we better all be thankful Jesus seeks to dine with sinners!"

Zacchaeus was changed that day. He was delivered. We know this because of what Jesus said: "And Jesus said to him, 'Today salvation has come to this house, because he also is a son of Abraham'" (Luke 19:9 NKJV).

Jesus recognized that salvation had come to Zacchaeus. No sinner's prayer is recorded. Sincerely praying a sinner's prayer is great! I offered one in chapter one, but there is not one in this story. Yet Jesus acknowledges the salvation of the former thief. Why? Because Zacchaeus was changed. Jesus saw fruit and knew it was coming from a new heart. "Then Zacchaeus stood and said to the Lord, 'Look, Lord, I give half of my goods to the poor; and if I have taken anything from anyone by false accusation, I restore it fourfold'" (Luke 19:8 NKJV).

Jesus spoke of Zacchaeus's faith and salvation after Zacchaeus demonstrated proof of repentance. Proof? The man who had only been interested in filling his pockets began to empty them. He sought to pay back those with whom he had abused his authority and stolen from. He also volunteered to give half his net worth to the poor. Zacchaeus's first fruit of repentance was generosity.

Suppose God were greedy and withholding. If that were the case, we would have no hope. Because God is giving, He gave His only Son so that we may have forgiveness, peace, and hope here on earth, followed by eternal life in heaven. He gives us good things. The Bible says, "Every good gift and every perfect gift is from above, and comes down from the Father of lights, with whom there is no variation or shadow of turning" (James 1:17 NKJV).

Notice that James states, "every good gift and every perfect gift." I am often amazed to hear how some charge God falsely.

When evil happens, many immediately point to God. And yet the Word reminds us that He is the giver of good and perfect gifts. Jesus reminds us, "The thief does not come except to steal, and to kill, and to destroy" (John 10:10 NKJV).

The devil is a thief; the opposite of our generous God.

Let's get Paul's perspective on the generosity of God. In Romans 8:31–32 (NKJV), Paul builds a strong case concerning God's open hand. He writes, "What shall we say to these things? If God *is* for us, who *can be* against us? He who did not spare His own Son, but delivered Him up for us all, how shall He not also freely give us all things?"

This is an argument from greater to lesser. If God did not withhold His Son, it's proof He will not withhold any need we have.

It's one thing to possess a lot. God does. It's all His. He is an abundant God.

> "If I were hungry, I would not tell you; For the world *is* Mine, and all its fullness." (Psalm 50:12 NKJV)

> Indeed heaven and the highest heavens belong to the Lord your God, *also* the earth and all that is in it. (Deuteronomy 10:14 NKJV)

> The earth is the Lord's, and everything in it. The world and all its people belong to Him. (Psalm 24:1 NLT)

Paul, further confirming the abundance of God, wrote, "And my God shall supply all your need according to His riches in glory by Christ Jesus" (Philippians 4:19 NKJV).

And Job also wrote, "'Who has given Me anything that I need to pay back? Everything under heaven is Mine'" (Job 41:11 NLT).

It's one thing to have abundant possessions. Again, God does. But the greater blessing is that He has an abundance and is generous. The man in the following parable had an abundance but was far from generous. Remember, he's the one who tore down barns to build bigger ones.

> Then He spoke a parable to them: "The ground of a certain rich man yielded plentifully. And he thought within himself, saying, 'What shall I do, since I have no room to store my crops.' So he said, 'I will do this: I will pull down my barns and build greater, and there I will store all my crops and my goods.'" (Luke 12:16–18 NKJV)

You may wonder, "What should he have done with his abundance?" Here is a thought: give some, even a lot, away. But he couldn't, or more accurately, wouldn't. So Jesus used this parable to reveal the sad story of those who live and die without ever experiencing the joy of having a grateful, generous heart. Today, we don't tear down barns and build larger ones. We rent storage buildings.

I have had multiple personal experiences that have helped me understand the danger of loving money. I will never forget sitting with a wealthy man and talking him out of taking his own life. Surrounded by what many believe would bring fulfillment, this desperate man searched for a reason to live. If peace was for sale, he could have bought it. But you cannot purchase what's not for sale, and peace is not. Praise God! He doesn't sell peace; He gives it.

Many years ago, I had a valuable experience with a man I had admired while growing up. He played a significant role in my life for many years. He touched the lives of many young people by providing opportunities they would have never had without his generosity. He began a battle with cancer toward the end of his life. Sitting in his office, he told me he had always dreamed of a million dollars in cash stacked on his desk. He then made it clear that, after his diagnosis, the stack of money was not appealing at all. He said, "If you placed a million dollars on that desk, I would turn my back on it." The longing for *more* lost its grip with his diagnosis. That little story has stuck with me for years. At the end of his life, when time was of the essence, the appeal of material things faded. Money and things took a nosedive on his priority list.

Another story has probably marked my life more than any concerning money. I went to the home of a well-known businessman in the county where I grew up. I was young in both life and ministry, and he was, on the other hand, I'm guessing, in his seventies.

As we walked around his house, it became clear that he had a specific goal. Entering a room, he said, "You see all this. This used to be all I lived for. Now I am an old man about to die and realize all that matters is my relationship with God and my family." But then he looked at me and said, "Don't ever let money ruin your life."

I will always be grateful for the wisdom he shared that day. I had (and still have) so much to learn, but his words penetrated my heart and mind. He left this world, but not before marking mine. I sense he knew he had little time on earth left, so he tried to warn a younger man to beware of walking the same path that he had.

Lastly, there was Roger James. He was a successful tree planter in my hometown. Healed miraculously by the Lord of cancer later in life, God used him to touch many. Before going home to be with the Lord, his name became synonymous with generosity. He lived with an open hand because he had such a generous heart. He could have torn down his barns to build bigger ones, but instead, he sought ways to give. His generous spirit was a witness to the cause of Christ. Many years after his death, I find myself admiring him, not because of his wealth, but because of his generosity. Generosity is much more attractive than wealth.

I do not know a joyful, greedy person. And neither do you. Greed in the heart produces a sour, ungrateful, and, too often, arrogant attitude. I'm confident there is no more significant turnoff to the Gospel than greed.

We know faith pleases the Lord. Hebrews 11:6 is proof of that. But did you know the same thing is said about generosity? Second Corinthians 9:7 (NKJV) states, "*So let* each one *give* as he purposes in his heart, not grudgingly or of necessity; for God loves a cheerful give."

This verse was written as Paul encouraged financial support for believers in Jerusalem. In that context, Paul revealed God's delight in cheerful giving. Are you a cheerful or reluctant giver? According to the text, God loves it when we cheerfully give. That's generosity. And without it, life is on sinking sand.

Windproof Challenge:
The Bible does not say, "The Lord loves those who think about cheerfully giving." Instead, it says He "loves a cheerful giver." The best remedy for greed is generosity. I believe this is one reason tithing is so important. Tithing causes us to deal with the issue of giving often. With tithing, we give from the

top each time we increase financially. This discipline keeps giving a constant in our lives.

There's probably more pushback concerning tithing than any other topic. Many say, "That's in the law, so it's not for today." Actually, tithing was a principle before the law was given to Moses. Abraham tithed, and he lived long before the law. It's certainly worth noting that Jesus approved of tithing (Matthew 23:23). Tithing is highly beneficial regarding generosity, but like any discipline, it can become legalistic. It does not have to, yet it can. If it has become legalistic, I challenge you to return to joyful giving today. But don't stop there. Allow generosity to become a lifestyle rather than an event. This act of obedience will help place your life on a firm footing and withstand the storms in life. Generosity is a critical ingredient to a strong foundation and, thus, to living a windproof life.

4

FORGIVENESS

I wrote this book to help believers *windproof* their lives, which can only happen through applying truth. So many are educated beyond their level of obedience. In other words, we tend to know what to do but refuse to do it. James wrote, "But don't just listen to God's Word. You must do what it says. Otherwise, you are only fooling yourselves" (James 1:22 NLT).

As believers in Christ, we know that harboring unforgiveness is wrong. I can't count the number of times someone has said to me, "I know I need to forgive, but I don't know how." The struggle is real and widespread. True forgiveness would solve most of the social unrest in our world today. But it's not natural to forgive; it's supernatural.

Metaphorically, unforgiveness is the giant many unsuccessfully fight. And this giant can no more be defeated without God than Goliath would have been without God empowering David. Like David, you can cut off the head of unforgiveness with God. But I must be honest with you; unforgiveness will win decisively without the Lord's strength.

Understanding the lengths God went to make atonement for our sins is essential. The action God took reveals His desire to forgive. His Son's shed blood, and subsequent death, was the only way. So the Father sent the Son to pay our ransom. No scripture captures this truth like John 3:16 (NKJV): "For God so loved the world that He gave His only begotten Son, that whoever believes in Him should not perish but have everlasting life."

We also looked at this verse in the chapter on generosity. Consider Jesus's promise of everlasting life because of the forgiveness made available to those who believe in Him. Christ purchased our forgiveness. This verse teaches that God is generously forgiving. What a thought!

I have often thought there is something we should tell everyone who is born again. They should know the time will come when they will be called upon to extend forgiveness to others in the same way they received it from God. It's not if but when. This fallen world, saturated with pride, greed, hate, etc., will offer everyone multiple opportunities to harbor unforgiveness.

We should not be surprised Jesus shared a powerful parable concerning forgiveness with Peter. Like so many, Peter battled with unforgiveness. This truth is revealed in his question to Jesus: "Then Peter came to Him and said, 'Lord, how often shall my brother sin against me, and I forgive Him? Up to seven times?'" (Matthew 18:21 NKJV).

It seems Peter had someone in mind when asking Jesus this question. Perhaps he had a repeat offender he struggled to forgive for multiple offenses. His question is understandable for sure.

The answer Jesus gave Peter is where the challenge lies. Peter was given no wiggle room. Jesus did not focus on the offense or who had hurt Peter. Jesus went straight to the point. Christ tells a parable that, in essence, reveals forgiveness must happen no matter how many times we are hurt. Again, no wiggle room. Using hyperbole, Jesus says, "I do not say unto you, up to seven times, but up to seventy times seven" (Matthew 18:22 NKJV).

The parable that followed tells the story of a man who had been forgiven an enormous debt but was unwilling to forgive someone else a lesser debt. The point is that if we have received abundant forgiveness from God, we must extend it to those who offend us.

The parable's conclusion reveals the seriousness of those who have accepted forgiveness from God but cling to unforgiveness in their hearts toward others. The last two verses state, "And his master was angry, and delivered him to the torturers until he should pay all that was due him. 'So my heavenly Father also will do to you if each of you, from his heart, does not forgive his brother his trespasses'" (Matthew 18:34–35 NKJV).

Notice the word "torturers." That's precisely what unforgiveness brings to the person who possesses it or, more accurately, is possessed by it. Also, Jesus shares the location where unforgiveness takes up residence. He says forgiveness, true forgiveness, comes from the heart.

Forgiveness is an accounting term. To forgive is to cancel a debt owed. It's true; when you harbor unforgiveness, you live like a person(s) owes you something. Because of words and/or actions, a person creates a debt in your heart. And guess what? You're the only one who can forgive it. And until you do, you're not free.

Many incorrectly assume that we forgive to set people who harmed us free. However, when we forgive, we are not setting them free; we are setting ourselves free. Lewis B. Smedes said, "To forgive is to set a prisoner free and discover the prisoner was you."

I remember preaching years ago about forgiveness and focusing on how forgiveness means "to cancel a debt." Someone came to me afterward and said, "Austin, remind them that if they leave ten cents worth of unforgiveness in their heart, the devil will gain interest on it." His words to me were profound and so true. To forgive, as God commands, means to cancel a debt, not almost cancel a debt.

On that note, let's go back to the cross. Jesus, His body agonizing in pain and soaked in blood, hanging between heaven and earth, displayed love as it had never been. Some say a person's last words are the most important they ever speak. It makes sense to me. And Jesus had some words to express in his final hours. "So when Jesus had received the sour wine, He said, 'It is finished!' And bowing His head, He gave up His spirit" (John 19:30 NKJV).

"It is finished!" The meaning of these words can get lost in translation. The Greek word used is "*tetelestai.*" This signaled that there would be no need for any more sacrifice for sin. His death was sufficient. Forgiveness was available for all people for all time because of His atoning death. This word was used by a servant to his master to let him know his work was completed. When a debt was paid to a merchant, the payer would receive a document stamped "Tetelestai." The word, in that context, meant "paid in full."

Jesus did not make a down payment at the cross. Our good works are not installments to make up for what Jesus did not do. To believe that is heresy of the highest order. No! He finished. He paid it all. There is nothing owed. Returning to my friend's thought, Jesus did not leave ten cents worth of sin to pay. He paid it all. He accomplished His mission. His work was complete. He sat down at the Father's right hand, not because He was tired but because He was finished!

But remember, we are to forgive as we have been forgiven. Paul writes in Ephesians 4:32 (NLT), "Instead, be kind to each other, tenderhearted, forgiving one another, just as God through Christ has forgiven you."

This verse raises the bar on forgiving others. It does not say to forgive like your pastor or like Paul. Instead, it states that we are to forgive as God has forgiven us through the work of Christ.

Everyone wants wide margins when it comes to the topic of forgiveness. Why? Because, for some reason, we believe our story exempts us from forgiving. We wrongly conclude that our particular story certainly warrants latitude in forgiveness. Indeed, we pridefully assume that God does not expect us to forgive such actions against us. This reasoning indicates that a person has drifted far from the cross. They've lost sight of the perfect Son of God, unrecognizable, hanging on a cross with His mother watching, as He paid the world's sin debt.

Sadly, many people will never get through the roadblock of unforgiveness. Imagine life as a long highway with many different experiences God has planned for you. The experiences include the works He has for you to do with the talents and gifts He has given you, relationships He has for you to grow, and various other opportunities. But there are roadblocks, and none are more significant than unforgiveness.

As I write this chapter of *Windproof,* I have been pastoring TruthPoint for well over twenty-five years and Cornerstone for well over a decade. These churches are in communities approximately twenty miles apart. As a pastor, I am convinced that unforgiveness is the number one struggle for believers, regardless of location. The atmosphere changes when this topic is addressed.

You may read this and think, "I will forgive them when they ask me to!" That's a dangerous approach to forgiving because there is a chance—and usually a good one—that you will not get an apology. For some reading this book, the person you have not forgiven is dead. Apologies may make forgiveness easier, but Jesus makes it possible.

I remember one of my first experiences with helping someone deal with forgiveness. I was an inexperienced pastor. A young mother came to my office to meet with me. She was broken, and it showed. Like so many, she had carried the weight of unforgiveness in her heart for many years. Her face told the story. There was a heaviness that was discernible.

Through many tears, she told me that, as a teenage girl, she was raped. The enemy had taken this experience and tortured her soul. Our conversation left my heart broken. I struggled for words to share. Finally, she told me she knew she had to forgive him but didn't know how.

We finished that meeting and followed up later. At that time, I remember the conversation going something like this: I asked, "Have you trusted Christ for the forgiveness of your sins?"

She answered yes.

And I, in essence, said, "If you had not trusted Christ, you would at least have every right to hate him. However, I wouldn't recommend unforgiveness under any circumstance.

But the moment you accepted Jesus, you forfeited that right to withhold forgiveness."

In part, our power to forgive others is found in the forgiveness we have received from God. You cannot give what you do not have. But because you have received grace, you can give it. More accurately, you must give it.

Though this young lady went through difficult times after our meeting, it did seem that I witnessed a miracle that day. I have often said it resembled watching someone drop chains from their hands and feet that have kept them bound. I believe something happened in her heart that she had desired for many years.

Seven years into our marriage, Jennifer and I faced a storm that revealed the weakness of our foundation. At that time, the average marriage in America lasted seven years, and almost seven years to the day, we discussed what lawyer we would use to divorce. Thank God we never made it to that lawyer's office.

I will never forget meeting with Jennifer after separating for quite a while. We determined we did want to attempt to work on our marriage and spend the rest of our lives together. But much healing was still needed, more than we could have imagined.

As God had it, there was a conference just south of Atlanta where a friend of mine, Ted Cunningham, was speaking. When we arrived, one of the first things a speaker said was, "We don't fix marriages." So I thought to myself, "Did I miss something? I brought my marriage here to be fixed." Like most men, I thought my marriage was like my vehicle. When my truck breaks down, I take it to the mechanic to fix it. So I reasoned that the two-day marriage conference would heal my broken marriage. But I soon learned that fixing a vehicle and a heart are as different as chalk and cheese.

The conference focused on the heart. A key verse used was Proverbs 4:23 (NLT), which states, "Guard your heart above all else, for it determines the course of your life."

In other words, the course of your life is determined by the condition of your heart. Likewise, in the context of marriage, the course of your marriage is determined by the condition of each spouse's heart.

Suffice it to say that Jennifer and I both had heart issues, but not the same. Our strongholds differed. But our marriage did not have a chance until God broke those strongholds and healed our hearts.

My heart was full of pride and unforgiveness. I will deal with pride in another chapter, so I will not expound much here. I will only say that, like so many problems, pride was the source of my problem. Prideful people are easily offended and, thus, unforgiving; more on that later.

Let's refocus on unforgiveness. This cancer of the soul is difficult to remove once it sets in. It petrifies. The best thing to do is deal with it quickly. I suppose this is the reason Paul says, "'Be angry, and do not sin': do not let the sun go down on your wrath, nor give place to the devil" (Ephesians 4:26–27 NKJV).

The New Living Translation translates these verses. "And 'don't sin by letting anger control you.' Don't let the sun go down while you are still angry, for anger gives a foothold to the devil" (Ephesians 4:26–27 NLT).

I once heard John Maxwell talk about the importance of keeping short accounts. Far too many have a ledger of unforgiveness accounts dated decades back. If that is you, the enemy no longer has a foothold; he has a stronghold. It will go deeper if you do not deal with the root of bitterness.

Now, back to my story. The stronghold in my heart was bitterness. It was strangling me, and I knew it. Because of the root of bitterness in my heart, I battled all kinds of emotional issues. I certainly believe it caused physical problems in my body as well. I tended to be unloving and even more vulnerable to being unlovable. Because of my position as a pastor, I dangerously found ways, for the most part, to hide it in specific settings. But home was a different story.

Then I received a call from a neurosurgeon's office. At the time, I did not have a neurosurgeon, or at least I didn't know I did. That sounds strange, but it's true. I reflected on this experience in the chapter on prayer because it had a profound impact on my life. I had developed a slight twitch in my face, and a neurologist performed an MRI. Somehow, the neurologist's office did not inform me of the results. They did, however, contact a surgeon. When the surgeon's secretary called, she said, "I am calling to schedule your brain surgery." I politely told her I didn't have a neurosurgeon, so she might have been trying to call my father since we have the same name. She assured me they had the right person and that I needed to get to my neurologist for an explanation as soon as possible.

The MRI revealed a tumor the size of a peach near the stem of my brain and would require immediate surgery. At the time, whether it was malignant was inconclusive, which could only be determined by removing it. However, its massive size and proximity to vital nerves were not in doubt.

In a matter of days, I was in Augusta, Georgia, under the care of a brilliant, extremely caring neurosurgeon, Dr. John Vender. He quickly scheduled the surgery. At the age of forty-six, I learned a valuable lesson. One of the most beneficial experiences for some of us is walking up to death's door, getting turned away, and having the chance to live with a new appreciation for life.

Before being diagnosed with the brain tumor, I had journaled about unforgiveness eating at my soul. I remember, in desperation, pouring my heart out on the keys of my computer. At that point, I was volatile. And the volatility was showing up in ways, looking back, that harmed others.

There's a quick lesson to learn here. If you are unforgiving toward anyone, it will eventually affect your relationships with everyone. Remember, according to Proverbs 4:23, your heart is the source of your life. And if your heart is full of bitterness and unforgiveness, it will show in your day-to-day life. It's been said that we bleed on those who did not cut us. This statement is especially true when it comes to unforgiveness.

Facing enormous uncertainty concerning my life made me deal with the unforgiveness in my heart. It was somewhat confusing to me to hear people say why I had the tumor. Some said God put it there. Others said the devil put it there. Dr. Vender told me it had been there since I was in my mother's womb, which makes me believe it was because we live in a fallen world where sickness and death occur. I will let the theologians duke it out over the why. Let me tell you who used it though. God did. He used the tumor and its threat on my life to make me deal with issues in my heart. I like to say that Dr. Vender took a tumor out of my head, and God took bitterness out of my heart. I am not saying that it takes a tumor to remove bitterness, but in my case, it did. Unforgiveness had made me one of those mad Christians. I heard someone say, "I am still a Christian. I'm just not mad about it anymore."

The experience of genuinely forgiving has been challenging for me to explain effectively. But as I heard someone say once, "I'm afraid we get good at managing strongholds." The problem is that if you are managing a stronghold, you still have it. We have not been called to manage them; we have the power because of Jesus to destroy them. Paul wrote, "For the weapons of our warfare *are* not carnal but mighty in God for the pulling down of strongholds" (2 Corinthians 10:4 NKJV).

I often hear people say we should forgive and forget. I would like to address that statement. Forgiveness is more powerful than that. I do not believe it is necessary to forget the offense to determine if true forgiveness has happened. Instead, true forgiveness allows you to live free from the offense that occurred. Consider the words of Jesus concerning those who have hurt you: "But I say to you, love your enemies, bless those who curse you, and do good to those who hate you, and pray for those who spitefully use you and persecute you" (Matthew 5:44 NKJV).

It is not natural to fulfill these commands from Jesus. Instead, as stated earlier, it's supernatural. It's natural to curse back at those who curse you and hate those who hate you.

I will let you know how to get freedom from hatred and unforgiveness. Obey Jesus's command to love and pray for your enemies even if you don't feel like it. You won't feel like it in your flesh. Pray for the person (or people) specifically. If they have family, pray for them as well. It's incredible how God uses obedience to this command to work in our hearts. Go ahead. Try it!

Our criminal justice system is designed to remove certain freedoms from those who commit crimes. Judges and juries hear each case, determine guilt or innocence, and then, if needed, render appropriate judgment. Certain crimes guarantee the loss of privileges and freedoms. For example, people can lose their driver's licenses, the right to vote, and, in extreme cases, their lives.

Just as societal freedom can be forfeited, so can our spiritual freedom. And nothing robs spiritual freedom like unforgiveness.

The bondage associated with bitterness is torturous. This explains why unforgiveness is usually easily detectable in others. Perhaps as you read this, you are in prison, and it is constructed out of your bitterness.

After many years in ministry, I have concluded there is no greater bondage than that of legalism. It is cold and unforgiving. Legalists are far more interested in condemning the guilty than helping free them. No place in scripture shows this more than the story of the woman caught in adultery.

Remember, the Pharisees wanted her stoned. They could not wait to see her pay for her sin. Vain religion had ruined them and many since. Here is a simple principle to remember: a sure sign of legalism is unforgiveness. You can take that to the bank. These cold-hearted theologians demanded justice, not mercy, for the guilty woman. I love this story because they brought her to Jesus to die, but instead of death, she received life. She arrived at the feet of Jesus in bondage but left free. Accidentally, while trying to kill her, the Pharisees helped save her instead.

Have you ever watched someone be set free from prison? Their newfound freedom is overwhelming as they walk and often run from the confines that have held them. Finally, the prison is behind them, and opportunity is before them. The shackles and bars are gone. Wonderful experiences of freedom await.

The experience of spiritual freedom is even greater. Being free from the bondage of unforgiveness releases one from the internal chains that hinder its captives from the experiences and opportunities God has planned for them. This explains why some held in physical prisons are free while others living in mansions are in spiritual prisons.

I realize some who read this book will have experienced painful abuse. Whether sexual, verbal, or physical, the abuse left you wounded and unforgiving. Others have been abandoned by someone who stood at an altar and repeated sacred vows to you. And some will have been neglected, overlooked, bullied, or severely hurt by gossip. Regardless of how, most, if not all, who read this chapter have been given opportunities to harbor hate. But here's the good news. No matter your experience, you do not have to live another day in the unmerciful grip of unforgiveness.

There are a few days I will never forget in this life. Unfortunately, the memories of most days have faded with time. I can't recall a memory from many of the thousands of days I have lived. Yet I remember the day I was born again by the Spirit of God. I remember the day I married my beautiful wife, Jennifer. I vividly remember getting the call about my MRI that revealed a brain tumor. Even more so, I remember the day I listened to a voicemail informing me that the tumor was not malignant. I will never forget dancing with my oldest daughter, Alora Gail, at her wedding reception. I suppose there are more days I could list, but I will not for the sake of time.

But I do want to list one more. With pristine clarity, I remember when the chains of unforgiveness fell from my heart. I had forgotten such freedom was possible. The darkness had blinded me.

Not many days after forgiveness took place and the tumor was removed from my brain, I was reminded of how evident the freedom that comes with forgiveness is. My middle daughter, Kee Kee, and I were riding somewhere together. She was around twelve years old at the time. She looked at me and said, "Daddy, that brain tumor was good for our family." I know that makes some people cringe theologically. She was not drawing theological conclusions, so settle down. She had simply made an accurate observation at such a young age. She essentially said, "Daddy, your surgery took more than a tumor out of you, and whatever it was is making a difference in our family." I knew what she meant. And she was right. More than a brain tumor was removed, something much more dangerous than a brain tumor—unforgiveness.

Windproof Challenge:
Today could be your day. Remember those special days I mentioned earlier? You most likely have some too. But I can assure you, one of the most unforgettable days of your life will be the day you, by the grace of God, open the prison door of bitterness and let yourself go free. You can't windproof your life by knowing you should forgive. Instead, you must forgive. Forgiving the person(s) does not mean what they did to you was OK. That's a lie the enemy wants to sell you to keep you in prison. Don't buy it.

Look at the ledger of unforgiven offenses in your heart and mind. Now, get a glimpse of the cross in your mind's eye. See Jesus's blood-soaked body hanging there to pay for your sins and hear His words, "Father, forgive them, for they know not what they do" (Luke 23:34 NKJV).

Now, take one last look at the list of wrongs and cancel the debt. It won't set them free, but it will you and will enable you to become windproof.

5

HUMILITY

None of the windproof principles this book deals with are more essential than humility. Humility is an attitude, just like arrogance. We are arrogant and prideful in our flesh, poor witnesses for our meek Savior. Humility results from living with a proper fear of the Lord and being dependent on Him. Pride leads people to believe that God depends on them or, at the very least, that they do not need God.

This book's primary goal is to help readers develop a firm footing amid the howling winds of the world. Remember, Jesus taught that a person builds his life on the rock by hearing and applying the truth. But unfortunately, those building on the sand often know the truth; they just don't obey it.

Nothing is as destabilizing to one's life as pride. Prideful people like to give the appearance that they are stable and secure. They're not though. Pride produces an arrogant attitude. Humility leads to confidence that derives from dependence on the Lord. Proverbs 14:26 (NKJV) states, "In the fear of the Lord *there is* strong confidence, And His children will have a place of refuge."

The prideful are not confident; they're arrogant. On the other hand, the humble are not arrogant; they're confident. Humble people are aware that their weakness gives room for the manifestation of God's strength (2 Corinthians 12:9).

Jesus was humble. This critical trait made Him approachable. When inviting the hurting and downcast to come to Him, Jesus mentioned His humility as a reason they could approach Him without hesitation. "Then Jesus said, 'Come to me, all of you who are weary and carry heavy burdens, and I will give you rest. Take my yoke upon you. Let me teach you, because I am humble and gentle in heart, and you will find rest for your souls. For my yoke is easy to bear, and the burden I give you is light'" (Matthew 11:28–30 NLT).

This was an invitation to the hurting. So to encourage them to come, Jesus described Himself as "humble and gentle." Humility makes communication with us easy. Pride makes us prickly, thorny, difficult to talk to, self-centered, and unapproachable. Yet amazingly, though Jesus was God wrapped in flesh, He was approachable.

The apostle Paul pointed the believers in Philippi to the humility of Christ. In Philippians 2:3–4 (NKJV), he writes, "*Let* nothing *be done* through selfish ambition or conceit, but in lowliness of mind let each esteem others better than himself. Let each of you look out not only for his own interests but also for the interests of others."

Paul's challenge would continue, but let's examine these commands briefly. First, Paul was likely addressing a known problem among the Philippians. Anywhere there's a group of people, there is the possibility (or probability) that dissension will happen. The most potent cure for strife and discord, though, is humility.

Paul highlights selfishness. I've often said that the problem with pride is that it is a mother sin. You may wonder what that means. Like a mother, pride gives birth. It gives birth to selfishness, jealousy, unforgiveness, etc. That's why most, if not all, of our relationship problems could be solved with a healthy dose of humility.

I mentioned earlier the crisis Jennifer and I experienced after seven years of marriage. God's healing of our broken hearts and home created a ministry for married couples. The miracle He performed was not just for us. We will forever believe He healed us to use us to bring healing to others. I mention that again because we can tell you from experience what pride will do to a marriage. The first seven years of our marriage serve as exhibit A.

Paul addressed a crucial issue concerning relationships when writing about selfishness and conceit. The definition of *conceit* is "excessive pride in oneself." Selfishness is an offspring of pride and is disastrous to relationships, especially marriage, but also beyond. Furthermore, conceited people are manipulative, subtly seeking ways to use and even abuse others. And because selfishness is always rooted in pride, its only cure is humility. Paul will get to that.

Next, Paul writes, "Have this attitude in yourselves which was also in Christ Jesus" (Philippians 2:5 NASB).

After giving the command, "*Let* nothing *be done* through selfish ambition or conceit," Paul presents an example; his example is Jesus. Interestingly, the word *attitude* is translated in some versions of scripture as "mind." So your attitude is the direct result of your thoughts and beliefs. When I come home sometimes with a less than stellar attitude, my youngest daughter, Dempsey Anna, will say, "Daddy, lose the tude!" If you think it's hard being a preacher's kid, you should try being a kid's preacher!

After the command to have the attitude of Jesus, Paul launches into profound theology for a few verses. First, he reminds the reader that Jesus was God. If anyone had reason to be prideful, it was Jesus, but He wasn't. "Though He was God, He did not think of equality with God as something to cling to" (Philippians 2:6 NLT).

The J.B. Phillips New Testament translates this verse, "For He, who had always been God by nature, did not cling to His prerogatives as God's equal."

What was Paul's point? Simply, Jesus was God. He didn't think He was; He *was*. And being God in the flesh, He was humble. He further writes, "but made Himself of no reputation, taking the form of a bondservant, *and* coming in the likeness of men. And being found in appearance as a man, He humbled Himself, and became obedient to *the point of* death, even the death of the cross" (Philippians 2:7–8 NKJV).

There you have it. Paul challenged the believers to have a humble attitude, as Jesus did, which allowed Him, God in the flesh, to die on the cross willingly for others.

Of course, Jesus's humility was on display during His ministry. He constantly served others, so much so that John 21:25 (NKJV) states, "And there are also many other things that Jesus did, which if they were written down one by one, I suppose that even the world itself could not contain the books that would be written. Amen."

His works were the result of humility. As God, He could have demanded that everyone serve Him. But instead, because of humility, Jesus constantly served others.

Jesus's humble attitude was on full display the night He was betrayed. Even then, He demonstrated humility with the world's weight on His shoulders. Remember, humility, according to Paul, includes focusing on the needs of others. "Let each of you look out not only for his own interests, but also the interests of others" (Philippians 2:4 NKJV).

Think about it. If Jesus had been prideful and self-centered, He would have never died on the cross for people who hated Him.

But another act succinctly demonstrates Christ's humility. Its symbolism is rooted in a well-known custom in biblical times. Many homes had servants responsible for fulfilling the humble task of washing feet. Due to the Middle Eastern climate, it was common for people to go barefoot or wear sandals. This menial task of foot-washing was often designated to the lowest of servants and women in keeping with the day's culture.

On the night of Jesus's betrayal, He led His disciples to a room to observe Passover. At that time, He spoke to them about the significance of His broken body and shed blood. Then He gave them bread and wine to symbolize the sacrifice He would make, and His church, to this day, observes the Lord's Supper so that the memory of the cross does not fade. But that was not the only symbolism Jesus used that night.

Interestingly, the upper room was also the setting of an argument. The disciples had a dispute over who was the greatest. Why do we get consumed with being the greatest? Pride. And in one of Jesus's most crucial hours, His disciples had a feud fueled by pride. Are you in a pride-fueled feud today?

Remember the story from the Introduction about the falling out between me and my pastor friend? When telling this story to the churches where I'm the pastor, I tell them the statute of limitations has run out (so they can't fire me for my actions).

Of course, the pride that caused the fight became our primary barrier until I attended the Bible conference, and the Lord deeply convicted my heart. I knew I was to initiate the makeup meeting. I thought, "But I did not start the feud." That didn't matter. What mattered was humbling myself and obeying the Lord; thankfully, I did, and mutual humility saved our friendship. I love him, and he loves me.

Let's go back to Jesus in the upper room. Like my pastor friend and I, the disciples experienced a conflict fed by pride. But Jesus had an object lesson on humility. With a towel and water bowl, he displayed humility in high definition.

Think about it. With all power in His hands, the Son of God used those hands to wash the feet of Peter, who would soon deny Him, and Judas, who would betray Him. You talk about humility! Jesus deserved for His feet to be washed, but a humble person is not interested in what he deserves but in the needs of others.

Titles and positions are so attractive to the prideful. Unfortunately, this attitude usually leads to a "serve me" mentality. Jesus was the King of kings and Lord of lords. The Bible says He has "All authority" (Matthew 28:18 NKJV). But He washed feet. He served others. He did not demand others serve His every need because of His title, "King of kings." Why? Because He was "gentle and lowly in heart" (Matthew 11:29 NKJV).

Humility is the great restorer of broken relationships. Through the years, I have talked with more hurting, angry couples than I can count. Not all have successfully gotten to the other side. If you were to ask me, "What's the main difference between couples that make it and those that don't?" Pride often builds a wall in one or both hearts, ultimately leading to destruction. Jimmy Evans has it right when saying, "The best marriages are made of two servants in love."

I remember a couple coming to my office. I did not know them then, but they have since become friends. But I must say, their story painted a picture of hopelessness. The pain was raw. There's no doubt about it. Pride could not have saved their marriage. Had pride set in, divorce would have been inevitable. But humility came to the rescue. Each of them humbled themselves and witnessed a miracle. Years later, I look out many Sundays and see them sitting together in church. The thought goes through my mind, "That's what mutual humility can do."

Much has been made in recent years about leadership. There are conferences galore in the Christian world on the topic. And to be sure, many of these conferences have contributed significantly to the cause of Christ. It is helpful for older, wiser leaders to share wisdom with aspiring young leaders.

But what is leadership? Or what makes a great leader? I do not doubt the answer to the second question. Simply, it's humility. This is precisely the truth Jesus was conveying in Luke 22. He states, "Who is more important, the one who sits at the table or the one who serves? The one who sits at the table, of course. But not here! For I am among you as one who serves" (Luke 22:27 NLT).

Using the simple illustration of a dining experience, Jesus redefined leadership from the world's perspective. The most outstanding leaders have humble servants' hearts. Those impressed with titles and positions believe it is beneath them to serve others. But true leaders are humble and desire to serve rather than be served. No task is beneath a Christ-like leader. As a true leader's position changes, he may not have to clean the toilets anymore, but he is more than willing to. Why? Because of humility.

At its core, humility is living in recognition of God's authority. As mentioned at the beginning of this chapter, humility results from being dependent on the Lord. Humility is the result of living with a proper fear of God. The humble person lives with an exalted view of God, which leads to an appropriate view of oneself.

At a specific point in Israel's history, the people demanded for themselves a king. Discontented, they wanted what other nations had. "Then all the elders of Israel gathered together and came to Samuel at Ramah, and said to him, 'Look, you are old, and your sons do not walk in your ways. Now make us a king to judge us like all the nations'" (1 Samuel 8:4–5 NKJV).

God was not pleased with their request. "And the Lord said to Samuel, 'Heed the voice of the people in all that they say to you; for they have not rejected you, but they have rejected Me, that I should not reign over them'" (1 Samuel 8:7 NKJV).

So guess what? A king they wanted, so a king they received.

The first king of Israel was named Saul. He looked like a leader and was received gladly by the people. "So they found him and brought him out, and he stood head and shoulders above anyone else. Then Samuel said to all the people, 'This is the man the Lord has chosen as your king. No one in all Israel is like him!' And all the people shouted, 'Long live the king!'" (1 Samuel 10:23–24 NLT).

Sometimes, when you get what you want, you do not want what you get. The people wanted Saul. Because he was their first king, times were exciting. But everything that begins well doesn't end well, especially when pride shows up. If you want to see how prideful he became, read 1 Samuel 15:12 (NLT), "Early the next morning Samuel went to find Saul. Someone told him, 'Saul went to the town of Carmel to set up a monument to himself; then he went to Gilgal.'"

How much pride does it take to build a monument to honor yourself? A lot! Others should bestow monuments with special recognition. Proverbs 27:2 (NLT) says, "Let someone else praise you, not your own mouth — a stranger, not your own lips."

There's something that doesn't feel right about honoring oneself with monuments. But that's what pride does. Prideful people must be noticed and recognized even if they must initiate it. Here is a thought: If you have to erect a monument to yourself, you don't deserve it. Eventually, pride cost Saul his position and, ultimately, his life. He could not handle the blessing. Like so many, the benefits given to him led to pride rather than humility. If you want to reveal the true character of someone, you don't have to take all they have; just give them more than they ever had. I'm reminded of what the Bible says about another king, Uzziah, in 2 Chronicles 26:16 (NLT): "But when he had become powerful, he also became proud, which led to his downfall."

Saul had not always been prideful, though. According to scripture, there was a time when he was humble. But as stated previously, the power and prestige of being king, to put it mildly, inflated his ego. So when Samuel, the prophet, confronted Saul, he reminded Saul of a time when his heart was different. "So Samuel said, 'When you *were* little in your own eyes, *were* you not head of the tribes of Israel? And did not the Lord anoint you king over Israel?'" (1 Samuel 15:17 NKJV).

There had been a time when Saul was little in his own eyes. God was once big in Saul's eyes, which gave him a proper perspective of himself. But fame and fortune cracked the door in his heart and in walked pride.

The list of those who have become big in their own eyes and paid the price is endless. My name is on that list. Is yours? I'm reminded of an article by Maureen Cleave about John Lennon, lead singer of the Beatles, in 1966. Lennon is quoted as saying, "Christianity will go. It will vanish and shrink. I needn't argue about that; I'm right and I'll be proved right. We're more popular than Jesus now; I don't know which will go first—rock 'n' roll or Christianity."

When making this statement, Lennon was undoubtedly drunk on pride and perhaps high on other substances.

Thomas Andrews built the *Titanic*, whose demise is well documented. The gigantic vessel's attention before its voyage undoubtedly filled Andrews with pride. In an interview about his grand creation, Andrews stated, "Not even God can sink it."

The ship's bow now rests on the bottom of the sea at 41°43'57" N 49°56'49" W, 400 nautical miles from Newfoundland, Canada.

God blesses the humble. James writes, "Humble yourselves in the sight of the Lord, and He will lift you up" (James 4:10 NKJV).

These words are similar to those Jesus spoke. But Jesus had an additional principle: "And whoever exalts himself will be humbled, and he who humbles himself shall be exalted" (Matthew 23:12 NKJV).

Peter also speaks about the blessing that comes with humility: "God resists the proud, But gives grace to the humble. Therefore humble yourself under the mighty hand of God, that He may exalt you in due time" (1 Peter 5:5–6 NKJV).

James reminds the reader that God will lift you up if you humble yourself. And Peter says that in due time, God exalts the humble. Look closely at these verses along with the words of Proverbs 22:4 (NKJV): "By humility *and* the fear of the Lord *Are* riches and honor and life."

The Bible is clear: God unquestionably blesses the humble. His word leaves no doubt that the humble heart is fertile ground for God's blessings.

Remember, pride is destructive. The Proverb writer states, "Pride *goes* before destruction, And a haughty spirit before a fall" (Proverbs 16:18 NKJV).

Notice pride is associated with destruction. Friendships, churches, marriages, and various organizations are destroyed by pride, so you can rest assured that pride has an eroding effect on life's foundation.

What was Satan's great sin? Pride. It's safe to say we are no more like the devil than when we are prideful. Once known as Lucifer, Satan was among the greatest of God's created angels. It is believed that Ezekiel described the fall of Satan: "You *were* the seal of perfection, Full of wisdom and perfect in beauty. You were in Eden, the garden of God; Every precious stone *was* your covering" (Ezekiel 28:12–13 NKJV).

Later, in verse 15, Ezekiel pens, "You *were* perfect in your ways from the day you were created, Till iniquity was found in you" (Ezekiel 28:15 NKJV).

Then the fall is described: "Your heart was lifted up because of your beauty; You corrupted your wisdom for the sake of your splendor; I cast you to the ground, I laid you before kings, That they might gaze at you" (Ezekiel 28:17 NKJV).

While these words were addressed to the king of Tyre, they seem to describe Satan ultimately. Whether you read this as written about an earthly king, Satan, or both (as I do), the truth remains that pride brought them down. Notice the words of Ezekiel 28:17, "Your heart was lifted up because of your beauty." Their blessing became their curse. How many have been puffed up with pride because of their beauty, wealth, or power? Too many.

Isaiah wrote about the fall of Lucifer. It is a little lengthy but worth reading:

> "How have you fallen from heaven, O shining star, son of the morning! You have been thrown down to the earth, you who destroyed the nations of the world. For you said to yourself, 'I will ascend to heaven and set my throne above God's stars. I will preside on the mountain of the gods far away in the north. I will climb to the highest heavens and be like the Most High.' Instead, you will be brought down to the place of the dead, down to the lowest depths." (Isaiah 14:12–15 NLT)

Notice how Satan, because of pride, was self-promoting. He said, "I will ascend," "I will preside," and "I will climb." He said, "I will be like the Most High." And what did it get him? He was cast out of heaven but still has lower to go. According to Revelation 20, the worst is yet to come. John wrote, "The devil, who deceived them, was cast into the lake of fire and brimstone where the beast and the false prophet *are*. And they will be tormented day and night forever and ever" (Revelation 20:10 NKJV).

Pride is so costly. Ultimately, it will have taken Satan from the highest heaven to the lake of fire. Why? Because pride always takes us downward.

I'm convinced that one of the most beneficial experiences we are given in this life is brokenness. It hurts but it helps. Brokenness and humility go hand in hand. Brokenness precedes humility, and often, heartache precedes brokenness. Usually, the humble have a story, a testimony of their road to humility. Some have an appointment with brokenness and do not know it. God can and will humble the prideful. Jesus said, "And whoever exalts himself will be humbled, and he who humbles himself will be exalted" (Matthew 23:12 NKJV).

I have heard people arrogantly boast of being self-made. Usually, this is said by someone who does not want you to think they have had any help in attaining what they have acquired. This self-sufficient attitude reeks of pride. The arrogant are unaware of the instability of the pedestal of pride on which they are standing.

The prideful do not believe they need God. For this reason, in my opinion, pride is the main reason for the lack of prayer. Why would a church, dependent on slick methods, pray? Why would a deacon, more interested in religious power than lost souls, pray? Why would a pastor who has mastered plagiarism and an academic approach to sermon preparation pray? Prayer is at its best when the one praying is aware of his/her dependence on God.

There is no substitute for humility in the Christian life. Paul commands us to live with the attitude of Christ. Christ's attitude of humility led to His obedience and death on the cross for sinners. The prideful do not give much of anything to others; they especially will not give their life. But Jesus, with humility, did. He willingly laid down His life as an act of service.

The most beneficial life experiences remind us of our need for and dependence on the Lord. Some may read this and maintain their arrogance. You may defiantly reject your need for Him and keep your house on the sand. You can do that. Our gracious, good God gives you a choice. To your peril, you can continue, like Saul, to erect monuments to yourself. You can live the miserable life of placing yourself in the center of your world.

To build a rock-solid foundation in life, you must reject pride and embrace a humble attitude. Live in constant awareness of your need for God. Serve others. Walk into rooms, looking for ways to serve, not to be served. Keep a fresh image of Jesus washing the disciples' feet in your mind's eye. Better yet, never lose sight of Jesus hanging on the cross in humble obedience to His heavenly Father and paying for your debt.

Humility is the key to so many aspects of the Christian life. Humble people worship God. They understand their need for Him and are grateful. Humility is essential to service, yet prideful people seek to be served. The humble serve sacrificially, even joyfully. Of course, some full of pride commit acts of service, but they are motivated by recognition and applause. Someone unwilling to serve sacrificially lacks humility. Humility precedes obedience. Saul became prideful and did what he wanted, costing him the kingdom. Jesus, with humility, "became obedient to *the point of* death, even the death of the cross" (Philippians 2:8 NKJV). Micah 6:8 (NKJV) sums it up very well: "He has shown you, O man, what *is* good; And what does the Lord require of you But to do justly To love mercy And to walk humbly with your God?"

Windproof Challenge:
One of the most well-known Old Testament scriptures is 2 Chronicles 7:14 (NKJV). It begins, "if my people who are called by My name will humble themselves ....."

The verse lists the benefits of humbly seeking God's face in prayer. God said he would hear, forgive, and heal. But these blessings are all preceded by humility. Remember, humility precedes prayer because the humble live in constant awareness of their dependence on the Lord. Look again. It says, "humble themselves." First Peter 5:6 (NKJV) states, "Therefore humble yourselves under the mighty hand of God."

It's one thing to know you should humble yourself; it's another to do it. You *must* do it. Knowing you should and refusing to do so will lessen your resistance to the inevitable storms in life. Humility is essential for a firm foundation. There's no substitute for humility if you want your life to be windproof, so humble yourself today. You'll be glad you did.

6

LOVE

Years ago, while a student at Liberty University, I joined my parents in the mountains of North Georgia. After months of intense study, it was a welcomed getaway. While driving, we rode by the state fairgrounds and saw a sign advertising a concert by the country music group, Shenandoah.

I had always loved country music. How could a boy who grew up in deep South Georgia not? Daddy and I had ridden miles in the 1980s, listening to Merle Haggard, Alabama, and John Conlee. So a Shenandoah concert caught our eye, but we had no idea how God would use this concert.

Daddy had not known the Lord long, and my call to ministry was fresh. We like to joke that since God changed

Daddy's heart, he even cries at Walmart openings. And our experience at the Georgia State Fairgrounds certainly left us teary-eyed.

Marty Raybon was Shenandoah's lead singer. I did not know him, but he has come and shared his testimony at TruthPoint in recent years. We had no idea when we bought our tickets that night that Marty had, after a long bout with addiction, given his life to Jesus Christ. We only knew we wanted to hear him sing "Moon Over Georgia." But it would get much better than that.

Marty introduced one of the band's hits, "I Want To Be Loved Like That." He made a few remarks about love and said, "But I want you to know that the greatest love ever was displayed on a cross two thousand years ago by Jesus Christ." I will never forget it. Marty's humility and boldness deeply moved us. A holy hush settled over that building, and hundreds, if not thousands, heard the most wonderful news known to man through the lips of a country music singer. The fans did not come to listen to those words, but listen they did. And they heard the best news available to this world loud and clear.

There's no way to live a windproof life without understanding God's love for you, loving Him, and loving others. Love is the key. When describing God, John simply wrote, "He who does not love does not know God, for God is love" (1 John 4:8 NKJV).

This is the last truth the devil wants you to believe. With his fiery darts, the enemy seeks to convince us that God lacks compassion. So why was Paul so stable? How did he withstand innumerable battles and trials? He was unquestionably windproof. But how? He wrote,

> In everything we do, we show that we are true
> ministers of God. We patiently endure troubles

and hardships and calamities of every kind. We
have been beaten, been put in prison, faced angry
mobs, worked to exhaustion, endured sleepless
nights, and gone without food. (2 Corinthians
6:4–6 NLT)

Paul moved from one battle to another with undiminished
passion. How? What was his secret? The good news is that
it's not a secret. Paul had a great understanding of God's love,
but even he acknowledged that the love of God is so vast that
it "passes knowledge." Ephesians 3:19 (NLT) states, "May
you experience the love of Christ, though it is too great to
understand fully. Then you will be made complete with all the
fullness of life and power that comes from God." In Romans
8:37–39 (NLT), Paul wrote,

No, despite all these things, overwhelming
victory is ours through Christ, who loved us.
And I am convinced that nothing can separate
us from God's love. Neither death nor life,
neither angels nor demons, neither our fears
for today nor our worries about tomorrow—nor
even the powers of hell can separate us from
God's love. No power in the sky above or in the
Earth below—indeed, nothing in all creation
will ever be able to separate us from the love of
God that is revealed in Christ Jesus our Lord.

In my opinion, that's Paul's *secret*. Thankfully, he wrote
his secret in the best-selling book of all time, the Bible. Paul
knew a lot of truth, but none impacted his life more than his
understanding of grace—the unmerited love of God.

The great anthem of the church will always be "Amazing Grace." This hymn, written by John Newton in 1772, has stood the test of time and will no doubt continue. Newton was converted in part because of a violent storm off the coast of Ireland, which he experienced while slave trading. He called out to God, and God heard. Later, he penned the words that have touched millions.

> Amazing Grace, how sweet the sound
> That saved a wretch like me
> I once was lost, but now I am found
> Was blind but now I see
>
> Through many dangers, toils and snares
> We have already come
> T'was Grace that brought us safe thus far
> And Grace will lead us home.

Long before Newton's beautiful words were laid to paper, Paul, the humble apostle, wrote extensively about grace under the inspiration of the Holy Spirit. Grace was his focus. Like no other, he delved into grace and changed the course of history.

Grace is defined as "undeserved or unearned love." This helps explain the reason Paul was consumed with it. Paul was a legalist before being converted to Christ, believing God accepted him based on his performance and pedigree rather than God's love. That's a terrible way to live and an even worse way to die. In life, a works-based theology places people on shifting sand.

I do not want to spend too much time on works and grace here, but Paul spent much of his time battling the legalists he had once led. Works-based religion will forever be a battle the church must fight with the sword of scripture. Sadly, some in churches who claim to be evangelical will never know the liberty that comes with grace-based theology. Many incorrectly conclude that to be grace-based is to be weak on sin and watered down. These people live in more fear than they are willing to admit. Joy eludes them. Some believe they lose and regain their salvation multiple times a week. It's beyond sad. God does not forgive me because I'm good, but because He is good. Paul says it best in Romans 11:6 (NLT), "And since it is through God's kindness, then it is not by their good works. For in that case, God's grace would not be what it really is—free and underserved."

You can have the same confidence and boldness Paul had. His was rooted in understanding God's love. Paul loved the Lord, but his strength was found in the love he knew God had for him.

What motivated Paul to continue to press forward in the face of persecution and suffering? God's love. He was not motivated by guilt, pride, or fear. Paul writes, "For the love of Christ compels us" (2 Corinthians 5:14 NKJV).

To *compel* means "action caused by pressure." God's love drove Paul, and there is no greater motivation. That truth is captured best in the most well-known verse in the Bible: "For God so loved the world that He gave His only begotten Son, that whoever believes in Him should not perish but have everlasting life" (John 3:16 NKJV).

No question. Love motivated God to give His Son for sinners. I love that it says, "God so loved." But again, the last truth the devil wants you to grasp is the depth of God's love for you.

The most oft-repeated command in the Bible is some form of "Do not fear." Fear is a paralyzer. It stops us in our tracks spiritually. Satan plays the fear card repeatedly because it has been a successful weapon in his corrupt arsenal. Many who read this book are in fear's grip, but you do not have to remain there.

Ultimately, fear results from unbelief, mostly unbelief in God's love. If God were as unloving as some believe He is, we would have reason to be afraid. But because He is our loving heavenly Father, there is no reason to fear. John addresses this in 1 John 4:18 (NKJV): "There is no fear in love; but perfect love casts out fear."

Fear in the heart of a believer results from a lack of belief in God's love. Failure to correctly believe in grace leads to fear. If you struggle with fear and anxiety, no better Bible study is available than one on God's grace.

Some believe the devil's goal is to cause people not to believe in God. Even he knows that it is a difficult battle because of creation and its meticulous systems. The incredible organization of the universe could no more have happened by chance than dismantling a Timex watch into a hundred pieces, throwing it into the air, and having it land perfectly connected, showing the right time. So I am convinced that Satan is content to deceive people to misbelieve rather than disbelieve when it comes to God.

A.W. Tozer wrote, "What comes into our minds when we think about God is the most important thing about us." Although this statement has met resistance, I believe Tozer is undoubtedly on to something. Indeed, not believing in God is deadly, but thinking wrongly about Him can be equally, if not more, damaging.

Jesus made many startling statements during His time on Earth. For example, look at this exchange between Jesus and Philip: "Philip said to Him, 'Lord, show us the Father, and it is sufficient for us.' Jesus said to him, 'Have I been with you so long, and yet you have not known Me, Philip? He who has seen Me has seen the Father; so how can you say, Show us the Father?'" (John 14:8–9 NKJV).

Paul wrote in Colossians 1:15–16 (NKJV), "He is the image of the invisible God, the firstborn over all creation. For by Him all things were created that are in heaven and that are on Earth, visible and invisible, whether thrones or dominions or principalities or powers. All things were created through Him and for Him."

Is it any wonder Jesus infuriated the Pharisees? His claim to be God was more than they could bear. Maybe He was a gifted teacher or even a prophet, but His claim as God sent them over the theological edge.

So if you desire to know what God is like, look no further than Jesus. Study the Gospels. Read His words. Consider His actions. In doing this, you will see the heart of the Father. And no one has ever displayed grace like Jesus. No one.

Sometime back, a gentleman called me. He was kind and sincere, so this is not disparaging him. He told me he watches our local television program and that I had said something he disagreed with. He said that I said, "Jesus never preached grace." I did not remember saying those words, but to correct me, he quoted to me 2 Corinthians 12:9 (NKJV), "And He said to me, 'My grace is sufficient for you, for My strength is made perfect in weakness.'"

His point was excellent and well-taken. I ended the conversation by saying to him, "Sir, I do not doubt I said that, but if I did, I said something I do not believe. Because I believe Jesus is grace!"

We could examine many stories, but let's focus on one that contrasts Jesus with the legalists of His day and highlights His grace. Jesus in essence said if you want to know what God is like, look at Him (Jesus).

I referenced the story of the woman caught in adultery earlier in the book, but it's worth a second look. It reveals the sinful nature of people, the pride of legalists, and the love of God: "Then the scribes and Pharisees brought to Him a woman caught in adultery. And when they had set her in the midst, they said to Him, 'Teacher, this woman was caught in adultery, in the very act. Now Moses, in the law, commanded us, that such should be stoned. But what do you say?'" (John 8:3–5 NKJV).

Don't you know these graceless legalists were licking their religious chops? What would Jesus say? She was caught red-handed. They had Him right where they wanted Him. Or so they thought. Their plan backfired severely. They brought her to Jesus to put her on trial; instead, *they* were found guilty of hypocrisy. They reminded Jesus that Moses wrote in the law that she should be stoned. Then they made the mistake of saying to Jesus, "But what do you say?" (John 8:5 NKJV).

They surely regretted asking Him that question. He replied, "He who is without sin among you, let him throw a stone at her first" (John 8:7 NKJV).

They asked for it, and they got it. After Jesus wrote something in the ground (we don't know what), the Bible says, "Then those who heard *it*, being convicted by *their* conscience, went out one by one, beginning with the oldest *even* to the last. And Jesus was left alone, and the woman standing in the midst" (John 8:9 NKJV).

What a turn of events! The legalists brought her in to condemn her, and they left, having convicted themselves. I wonder if they thought, "Maybe that wasn't a good idea after all." But the last part of the story is the best. The Bible says, "When Jesus had raised Himself up and saw no one but the woman, He said to her, 'Woman, where are those accusers of yours? Has no one condemned you?'" (John 8:10 NKJV).

This would be humorous if it weren't so sad. The Pharisees were gone. Jesus put them on the run with His words. Their legalism was no match for His wisdom. The legalists came to highlight her sin, but the Light of the World shone on their wicked, cold, and hypocritical hearts.

Now, all that was left was the perfect, sinless Son of God and a woman who, though used by religious zealots, was guilty of committing adultery. Of course, we have already seen how the Pharisees treated the guilty woman, but what would God do?

Someone said, "The only One qualified to stone her that day did not." What a thought! If sinlessness was the prerequisite to stone her, Jesus qualified. He could have picked up a stone. But He didn't. Why not? Well, that's the point of this chapter.

Justice would permit Jesus to stone her, but grace prevailed. I'm reminded of Romans 5:20 (NKJV): "But where sin abounded, grace abounded much more."

He knew her sins were destined for His cross like the rest of the world's iniquity. She could have died for her sin, but she would be dying for a sin that Jesus Himself would soon die for. So here's the conclusion of the conversation: "She said, 'No one, Lord.' And Jesus said to her, 'Neither do I condemn you; go and sin no more'" (John 8:11 NKJV).

There you have it. That's grace. And remember, Jesus said that if you want to know what the Father is like, look at Him. Jesus did not come to condemn (John 3:17).

I guess it's safe to say we have all been represented by the guilty woman and loveless legalists. Like her, we have all blown it and needed grace. Like them, we have all been unwilling to extend grace. In the end, though, Jesus was like neither. He had never sinned, yet He did not have the arrogant attitude of the legalists. Instead, He had a heart full of love and forgiveness. He gave her what she needed, not what she deserved.

I have heard it for most of my ministry, so I might as well address it. Some will accuse those who focus on the grace of God as weak concerning sin. They say, "Well, you just believe a person can get saved and live it up in sin." If that's you, please look at the last line in John 8:11 (NKJV): "Go and sin no more."

So for all the modern legalists who love highlighting your righteousness and strong stance against sin, let down your pride for a moment and understand that most grace-filled preachers I know believe the opposite of what you conclude. Grace is not a reason to sin. Instead, it's the most compelling reason not to. Paul wrote, "Well then, should we keep on sinning so that God can show us more and more of His wonderful grace? Of course not! Since we have died to sin, how can we continue to live in it?" (Romans 6:1–2 NLT).

The story of the writing of the beloved song "The Love of God" is fascinating. Frederick Lehman wrote the song, but he was inspired by words found on a prison wall written by an inmate. Painters who came in to paint the prison walls wrote the words down before painting over them. It is believed that the deceased inmate was inspired to write the words because of his familiarity with an eleventh-century Jewish poem. Read the words slowly:

> Could we with ink
> the ocean fill
> and were the skies
> of parchment made,
> Were every stalk
> On Earth a quill,
> And every man a

scribe by trade,
To write the love of
God above
Would drain the
ocean dry.
Nor could the scroll
contain the whole,
Though stretched
From sky to sky.

For the most part, until now, this chapter has focused on God's love for us. Remember, a windproof life will be impossible without understanding God's love. Fear is a destabilizing force, but fear is no match for love. Reread this verse: "There is no fear in love; but perfect love casts out fear because fear involves torment. But he who fears has not been made perfect in love" (1 John 4:18 NKJV).

When we plunge into God's perfect love, it results in fearlessness.

What does God want most from us? Many responses come to mind. But look at the question again. The word "most" is the key. God wants to see faith, humility, generosity, and joy in the lives of His children, but again, what does He want the most? The answer to that question is easy to conclude. Jesus made it clear. More than anything else, God desires us to love Him.

Once again, this story involves the Pharisees. "Then one of them, a lawyer, asked *Him a question*, testing Him, and saying, 'Teacher, which is the great commandment in the law?'" (Matthew 22:35–36 NKJV).

There were hundreds of laws. The lawyer wanted the most important one. Which law carried the most weight? What mattered most? So Jesus answered the question and left no room for debate.

> Jesus said to Him, "You shall love the Lord your God with all your heart, with all your soul, and with all your mind. This is *the* first and great commandment. And *the* second is like it: You shall love your neighbor as yourself. On these two commandments hang all the Law and the Prophets." (Matthew 22:37–40 NKJV)

Wait for a second. Do you mean the most important commandment, according to Jesus, is not even taken from the Ten Commandments? No. It's not. Jesus quoted a passage from the book of Deuteronomy, known as the *Shema*. Shema means to "listen" or "hear." In Deuteronomy, Moses highlighted the importance of the command to love God. It is believed this was the first principle to be memorized by Jewish children.

Jesus also answered a question not asked. The lawyer only asked for the greatest commandment. However, Jesus gave him the second most important commandment. It also had to do with love. "You shall love your neighbor as yourself." Jesus even said, "And *the* second is like it," meaning they were similar. But the last sentence is most revealing: "On these two commandments hang all the Law and the Prophets."

Wow! Consider that statement: "On these two commandments hang *all* the Law and Prophets." What did He mean by that? He meant what He said. In a genuine sense, Jesus stated that even if you obey all other laws but don't love God and people, it doesn't count. Everything depends on obedience to the great commandment.

I remember being a guest preacher for a revival service many years ago. Before the service, the church had a fellowship supper. The hope of a fellowship supper is that believers can gather around a meal in sweet fellowship—a time of laughter and storytelling with the sweet aroma of home-cooked dishes.

When I arrived at the church, the pastor asked me to come to his office. I will never forget his words. He said, "Austin, at the fellowship supper tonight, a fight broke out, and I would not blame you if you wanted to leave and not preach."

I thought, "Nope. Sounds like revival is what we need!" But of course, the tension was palpable, and sadly, revival did not happen. The fight from the fellowship supper lingered and, thus, hindered.

I don't know if a greater oxymoron exists than "unloving church." When Paul addressed the Corinthian church in 1 Corinthians 13, he made startling statements. Consider a few verses:

> Though I speak with the tongues of men and of angels, but have not love, I have become sounding brass or a clanging cymbal. And though I have *the gift of* prophecy, and understand all mysteries and all knowledge, and though I have all faith, so that I could remove mountains, but have not love, I am nothing. And though I bestow all my goods to feed *the poor*, and though I give my body to be burned, but have not love, it profits me nothing. (1 Corinthians 13:1–3 NKJV)

Why did Paul write this? For weddings? Not specifically. The words are beautiful at weddings, but 1 Corinthians 13 is sandwiched into teaching about spiritual gifts, gifts used to serve one another in the local church. In essence, Paul stated that using spiritual gifts minus love equals nothing. That's plain from the text above.

The book of Revelation is fascinating. The apostle John penned this book that contains symbolism and prophetic truths, revealing insights that can invoke fear and comfort. Moreover, chapters 2 and 3 of Revelation reveal letters from Jesus to seven local churches in Asia Minor: Ephesus, Smyrna, Pergamos, Thyatira, Sardis, Philadelphia, and Laodicea.

Each of these churches received insight from Jesus concerning their specific fellowship. What if local churches individually received customized letters from Jesus, revealing His thoughts about our ministries and motives today? Pastors should teach from these short letters to bring encouragement and course correction in our churches. No one, and I mean no one, has keen insights concerning local churches like Jesus.

The first church Jesus addressed in the book of Revelation was the church in Ephesus. This metropolitan city was known for its debauchery. To the Greeks, the temple in Ephesus was known as the temple of Artemis. It was one of the seven wonders of the world. Her image, a woman with multiple breasts, was believed to have fallen from heaven.

God planted a church in this sin-sick city. One of the richest books in the Bible was written by Paul and directed to the Ephesian church. Paul spent three years teaching the Gospel in Ephesus. His letter to the church was subsequently written from a jail cell.

But Jesus also had a word for the Ephesian church. Though short, His letter was packed with powerful insights applicable today. He began by commending some of their actions but quickly confronted them. He referred to their love for truth and hard work as a church. He even recognized their patience. But after these commendations, He said, "Nevertheless I have *this* against you, that you have left your first love" (Revelation 2:4 NKJV).

Consider the word, "left." The Ephesian church had left its first love. That was only possible because Jesus had once been their first love. You can't leave where you have never been. There had been a time when their motive in ministry was love for God. But somewhere along the way, they left Jesus but did not leave the church.

How much did it matter that they no longer loved Jesus the most? After all, they were fulfilling their Christian duty. Did Jesus find any satisfaction in their commitment to doctrinal purity and good behavior even though they did not love Him the most? That's an easy question to answer. Jesus said to them, "Remember therefore from where you have fallen; repent and do the first works, or else I will come to you quickly and remove your lampstand from its place—unless you repent" (Revelation 2:5 NKJV).

Someone said, "You can believe right and behave right and not be right." The Ephesian church was a classic case of that truth. Jesus called them to repent. Their lack of love for Him was no light matter. If they did not return to Him as their first love, He would remove their lampstand, which would mean lights out. And a church that has no light is useless and numbered in days.

You see, you can sing "Amazing Grace" and no longer be amazed by grace. You can work in ministry and no longer love Jesus the most. You can preach, teach, sing, greet, usher, or fulfill several ministries in the church and not have Jesus as your first love. But remember this: He knows. He knows what you do and, perhaps more importantly, why you do it.

This chapter hopefully has reminded you that love is essential for a windproof life. Understanding God's love for us and, in turn, loving Him the most is necessary. John reminds us that our love is in response to His love. In other words, don't confuse who loved who first. We were lost and dead in trespasses and sin until He, motivated by grace, came looking for us. Receive God's love and love Him the most in return. Your life can be windproof, but not without love. "We love Him because He first loved us" (1 John 4:19 NKJV).

John 14 is one of the most beloved chapters in the Bible. It's packed with hope. In verse 15, Jesus said, "If you love Me, keep My commandments." Jesus connected love for Him to obedience to Him. You can't windproof your life without obedience to God—and love should be your motive.

Windproof Challenge:

I have a simple challenge from this chapter. Meditate on these verses of scripture about the love and grace of God. Remember, Satan wants to prevent you from understanding God's unconditional love. He knows this will lead to a fearful life. So here are some great verses of scripture:

> Yet in all these things we are more than conquerors through Him who loved us. For I am persuaded that neither death, nor life, nor angels nor principalities nor powers, nor things present nor things to come, nor height nor depth, nor any other created thing, shall be able to separate us from the love of God which is in Christ Jesus our Lord. (Romans 8:37–39 NKJV)

> He who does not love does not know God, for God is love. In this the love of God was manifested toward us, that God has sent His only begotten Son into the world, that we might live through Him. In this is love, not that we

loved God, but that He loved us and sent His Son *to be* the propitiation for our sins. (1 John 4:8–10 NKJV)

But God demonstrated His own love toward us, in that while we were still sinners, Christ died for us. (Romans 5:8 NKJV)

But You, O Lord, *are* a God full of compassion, and gracious, Longsuffering and abundant in mercy and truth. (Psalm 86:15 NKJV)

I have been crucified with Christ; it is no longer I who live, but Christ lives in me; and the *life* which I now live in the flesh I live by faith in the Son of God, who loved me and gave Himself for me. (Galatians 2:20 NKJV)

7

BE FILLED

Years ago, I bought a copy of a book titled *Forgotten God*. Francis Chan, the author, captured the truth in his title. His thesis was that the Holy Spirit, sometimes referred to as the third person of the Trinity, has generally been forgotten by the church. We worship God the Father, and we should. We focus on Jesus the Son, and we should. But the Holy Spirit is often ignored. Or if not ignored, many need to keep Him in their tight, neat, little theological boxes. But He won't fit.

No life is windproof without the presence of the Holy Spirit. Being filled with the Holy Spirit means God Himself is on location, yielded to, and bearing fruit no matter where the believer is or what they face. So when the storms in life blow in, while the world must do its best without God, believers have God's actual presence with them. Or more accurately, in them.

The Old Testament is replete with mentions of the Holy Spirit. He would show up for specific tasks. The Old Testament even speaks of some being filled with the Holy Spirit. Exodus 31:1–5 (NKJV) says,

> Then the Lord spoke to Moses, saying: "See, I have called by name Bezalel the son of Uri, the son of Hur, of the tribe of Judah. And I have filled him with the Spirit of God, in wisdom, in understanding, in knowledge, and in all *manner of* workmanship, to design artistic works, to work in gold, in silver, in bronze, in cutting jewels for setting, in carving wood, and to work in all *manner of* workmanship."

Remember, this is found in the book of Exodus, not Acts. Bezalel, filled with the Holy Spirit, was equipped with wisdom, understanding, and artistic skill.

And then there was Samson. He struggled morally. We may be in awe of his physical strength. But I often ask, "How great could he have been if he had not given into the flesh?" I'm not condemning him; I'm simply asking a question. Consider the work of the Spirit in Samson's life: "Now *to his* surprise, a young lion *came* roaring against him. And the Spirit of the Lord came mightily upon him, and he tore the lion apart as one would have torn apart a young goat, though *he had* nothing in his hand" (Judges 14:5–6 NKJV).

He defeated the lion not by his power but by the Spirit's power upon him. And of course, there's David. It should be no surprise that a man with such spiritual depth knew of his need for the Spirit of God. The young shepherd boy was fetched from tending sheep and anointed by Samuel as Saul's replacement. The Bible says something interesting about the Spirit of God and Saul: "But the Spirit of the Lord departed from Saul, and a distressing spirit from the Lord troubled him" (1 Samuel 16:14 NKJV).

This distressing spirit from the Lord reminds us of God's chastising hand toward the prideful and rebellious king. So much had been given to Saul, and much was required. He failed miserably and paid a high price.

I mention this because David knew the possibility of the Spirit departing from him. Remember, when David was good, he was good, but he was also, at times, good at being bad. I have often said it was not the giant over nine feet tall that David struggled with as much as it was a *five-foot, five-inch*, brown-eyed brunette named Bathsheba. In a moment of weakness, he saw her and sent for her. And what followed was terrible. A faithful husband and warrior (Uriah) lost his life, and David and Bathsheba lost a child.

Eventually, the prophet Nathan confronted David concerning his sin with Bathsheba. David repented, but his sin was costly. I'm not sure anyone knows where the saying "Sin will take you farther than you want to go, keep you longer than you want to stay, and cost you more than you want to pay" originated, but I suspect David would say amen to it.

I am grateful we have the psalm David wrote after Nathan's visit. No doubt, David's sin and its consequences led to brokenness. And David made a request in Psalm 51 that revealed his fear. Most likely, he knew that the Spirit of the Lord had left Saul, so he prayed, "Create in me a clean heart, O God, And renew a steadfast spirit within me. Do not cast me away from your presence, And do not take Your Holy Spirit from me" (Psalm 51:10–11 NKJV).

I do not believe David could bear the thought of living without the presence of the Holy Spirit. He knew the source of his joy and power. And while I do not believe God gives and takes His Spirit with New Covenant believers, David's request to God should remind us of our dependence on His Spirit.

A favorite Old Testament story for many, especially regarding revival, is the vision of the Valley of Dry Bones. Ezekiel was given a vision of death—dry bones scattered in a valley, signifying death where there was once life. Ezekiel wrote, "Then He caused me to pass by them all around, and behold, *there were* very many in the open valley; and indeed *they were* very dry" (Ezekiel 37:2 NKJV).

Interestingly, God commanded Ezekiel to preach to the valley of bones. But of course, you would have to be a preacher to appreciate the task Ezekiel was called to fulfill. It's one thing to preach to disinterested people; it's another to preach to bones. But preach he did.

Amid the vision, the Lord commanded Ezekiel to prophesy to the breath: "Also He said to me, 'Prophesy to the breath, prophesy, son of man, and say to the breath, "Thus says the Lord God: Come from the four winds, O breath, and breathe on these slain, that they may live"'" (Ezekiel 37:9 NKJV).

So Ezekiel did as he was commanded and prophesied to the breath. The word "breath" derives from the word, *ruach*. This is important to understand because it is the word in Genesis 1:2 (NKJV) for "Spirit": "The earth was without form, and void; and darkness *was* on the face of the deep. And the Spirit of God was hovering over the face of the waters."

So it is safe to conclude that Ezekiel preached to the breath, or Spirit, to breathe on the lifeless bodies in the valley. Then they became a mighty army because of the Spirit's power. "So I prophesied as He commanded me, and breath came into them, and they lived, and stood upon their feet, an exceedingly great army" (Ezekiel 37:10 NKJV).

While Ezekiel's vision was meant to prophesy Israel's revitalization, I fear many churches resemble it today. There is no life without the power of the Spirit. Sadly, many churches, even entire denominations, rarely mention the work of the Holy Spirit. As a result, churches are loaded with money, talent, and gifted leadership but no spiritual power. Why? Because there is little or no emphasis on the Holy Spirit.

Then there is Joel's prophecy. His prophetic words served as the text Peter preached to shed light on the Day of Pentecost. Joel wrote,

> "And it shall come to pass afterward That I will pour out My Spirit on all flesh; Your sons and your daughters shall prophesy, Your old men shall dream dreams, Your young men shall see visions.
>
> And also on *My* menservants and on *My* maidservants I will pour out My Spirit in those days." (Joel 2:28–29 NKJV)

Hundreds of years later, Jews worldwide gathered in Jerusalem to celebrate Pentecost; however, they had no idea what awaited them. God had placed a day on His calendar to fulfill Joel's prophecy.

> When the Day of Pentecost had fully come, they were all with one accord in one place. And suddenly there came a sound from heaven, as of a rushing mighty wind, and it filled the whole house where they were sitting. Then there

appeared to them divided tongues, as of fire, and *one* sat upon each one of them. And they were all filled with the Holy Spirit and began to speak with other tongues, as the Spirit gave them utterance. (Acts 2:1–4 NKJV)

Wow! The Holy Spirit was poured out with the sound of a tornado. The impact of the Spirit caused some in attendance to accuse the disciples of being drunk. The Bible says, "Others mocking said, 'They are full of new wine'" (Acts 2:13 NKJV).

This accusation gave Peter the perfect opportunity to address what was going on. They were not drunk with wine. Instead, they were under the influence of God's freshly poured-out Spirit.

But Peter, standing up with the eleven, raised his voice and said to them, "Men of Judea and all who dwell in Jerusalem, let it be known to you, and heed my words. For these are not drunk as you suppose, since it is *only* the third hour of the day. But this is what was spoken by the prophet Joel." (Acts 2:14–16 NKJV)

Peter then quoted Joel's prophecy and preached Jesus to the crowd. As a result, thousands became believers in Christ, the church was birthed, and the Holy Spirit ignited boldness and power that changed the world. The book of Acts shares the church's history, blazing with God's power from one city to another and one country to another with fearless passion and authority. And it was not because of slick programs. Instead, individuals and churches were powerfully propelled by the Spirit of God.

Now, back to the point of this book. God has made it possible for us to be windproof in this world. But it is not possible without the presence and power of the Holy Spirit. The first church faced constant persecution. Winds of opposition blew strong in the face of those early believers, yet they marched forward undeterred. I'm sure they quickly understood why Jesus had said to them, "Behold, I send the Promise of My Father upon you; but tarry in the city of Jerusalem until you are endued with power from on high" (Luke 24:49 NKJV).

The task ahead of them was too great to fulfill without the presence of God; therefore, they were wise to wait. They could have never impacted the world the way they did without the presence of the Holy Spirit. Without Him, they could not have resisted and pushed back the forces against them.

The Bible teaches that believers possess gifts, also known as the gifts of the Spirit. Spiritual gifts in local churches help bring strength and stability to believers. The gifts of the Spirit are God's way of the body of Christ ministering to itself. There is a windproof effect as believers serve fellow believers with gifts and talents given by God, which again is another reason to connect to a local church.

Consider Paul's words to the Ephesian believers: "Don't be drunk with wine, because that will ruin your life. Instead, be filled with the Spirit" (Ephesians 5:18 NLT).

The contrast here is clear. Being drunk with wine brings instability. Those intoxicated with alcohol are incoherent and unstable, far from windproof. In contrast, Paul commands us to be filled with the Holy Spirit. Why? What advantage is there to being filled with the Holy Spirit? I am glad you asked. But let's look at another vital truth before answering that question.

Jesus made a statement concerning the coming of the Holy Spirit that has given some pause, and it shouldn't. Instead, it should cause us to ask why Jesus would make such a statement. He said,

> "But now I go away to Him who sent Me, and none of you asks Me, 'Where are You going?' But because I said these things to you, sorrow has filled your heart. Nevertheless I tell you the truth. It is to your advantage that I go away; for if I do not go away, the Helper will not come to you; but if I depart, I will send Him to you." (John 16:5–7 NKJV)

That is one of those wow moments in the Word. How on earth could it be an advantage for Jesus to go away? Well, He answered that question. Jesus's ascension would precede the outpouring of the Holy Spirit. The latter would not happen without the former.

As mentioned earlier, the Holy Spirit was poured out on the Day of Pentecost. It was one of the most important days in history. Although it is not celebrated the same way as the birth (Christmas) or resurrection (Easter) of Jesus, it is nonetheless essential.

Consider these verses concerning the work of the Holy Spirit in the life of believers:

> And do not grieve the Holy Spirit of God, by whom you were sealed for the day of redemption. (Ephesians 4:30 NKJV)

> The Spirit Himself bears witness with our spirit that we are children of God. (Romans 8:16 NKJV)

The presence of the Holy Spirit in a person's life is proof of salvation. He seals us, providing security for the believer. He bears witness to our spirit, giving assurance that God is our Father regardless of our circumstances. But there is more.

I want to conclude this chapter by discussing the fruit of the Spirit. This book aims to help you windproof your life. I cannot think of a better way to withstand the world's winds than to be filled with the Spirit. He has everything you need to live a stable and secure life.

As Paul finished Galatians, he contrasted the works of the flesh with the fruit of the Spirit. Paul was a theological genius, filled with the Holy Spirit, and his masterful use of words to convey profound truth was certainly on display in Galatians. Look at the contrast he made:

> Now the works of the flesh are evident, which are: adultery, fornication, uncleanness, lewdness, idolatry, sorcery, hatred, contentions, jealousies, outbursts of wrath, selfish ambitions, dissensions, heresies, envy, murders, drunkenness, revelries, and the like; of which I tell you beforehand, just as I told *you* in time past, that those who practice such things will not inherit the kingdom of God. (Galatians 5:19–21 NKJV)

> But the fruit of the Spirit is love, joy, peace, longsuffering, kindness, goodness, faithfulness, gentleness, self-control. Against such there is no law. (Galatians 5:22–23 NKJV)

A casual glance at the "works of the flesh" shouts instability. Most of us have experienced the disastrous results of living in the flesh. Living life in the flesh means doing what I want, when I want, without regard for God or anyone else. Pride rules the fleshly life. Again, look at the mess the flesh produces. Our culture is being dismantled by the works of the flesh. And no politician nor political program can cure the flesh. Only Jesus can do that. These issues originate in the heart, internally. The world may have methods to alter behavior, but God changes desires, which leads to self-government. The difference couldn't be more significant.

Remember Doug Heard? You're probably aware by now of his profound influence on my life. Doug was a hero to me. As previously mentioned, he was known to be one of, if not the toughest, man in the county. As I remember, he had little experience with religion. Ironically, I believe this helped him become the incredible man of God he became. He did not have to detox from the influence cultural Christianity has on so many in the Bible Belt.

After a short conversation at my house, it was very apparent that God had gently but firmly grabbed his heart. Doug was born again that day. He humbled himself before the Lord in the living room of his home and became a different man. No matter how long I live, Jesus's impact on him will influence me.

I tell you about Doug because of our conversation in his truck years ago. I briefly mentioned this story earlier. This conversation is etched in my heart. He looked at me and said, "Brother Austin, Jesus changed my want-tos." I had never heard it put that way before, nor have I since. But Doug was conveying a truth revealed in the Bible. Paul wrote, "Therefore, if anyone *is* in Christ, *he is* a new creation; old things have passed away; behold, all things have become new" (2 Corinthians 5:17 NKJV).

That's the truth Doug was explaining. God had changed his heart. He desired different things than before. Doug acknowledged that God had done an inside job on him. His want-tos changed, and he had the fruit to prove it.

Doug's testimony is Exhibit A on the contrast between the works of the flesh and the fruit of the Spirit; these contradict each other. The works of the flesh destabilize and bring disaster to many lives. On the other hand, the fruit of the Spirit leads to the abundant life Jesus spoke of in John 10:10. So let's look at the fruit Paul lists.

The first word Paul uses is love. There's an entire chapter in this book dedicated to love, so clearly, love is essential to having a windproof life. Consider the opposite of love: hate and bitterness. I cannot think of anything that destabilizes and destroys more lives than hate. Paul reminds us that a life filled with the Spirit will produce love.

As mentioned in a previous chapter, I took a miserable journey for a season with bitterness in my heart. I can tell you firsthand that it was unsettling and destructive. Sadly, it caused instability not only for me but also for those close to me. Bitterness brings collateral damage. Some people who are not the intended target of your hatred will be impacted.

Love, on the other hand, brings stability. When your heart is full of love, you are not self-centered and self-absorbed. Forgiveness is more readily extended. Remember, the Holy Spirit is God. To be filled with Him is to be filled with love. And nothing has the stabilizing effect that love has.

Secondly, Paul mentions joy. He reminds us that joy is not a fruit of the flesh but the Spirit. Joy is not the same as happiness. Of course, happiness is good and desirable. There's no reason to pit happiness against joy. But they are not the same. Joy is deeper. Joy results from an abiding relationship with Jesus and is not dependent upon our circumstances. John 15 records the words of Jesus concerning the importance of abiding in Him. He said, "These things I have spoken to you, that My joy may remain in you, and *that* your joy may be full" (John 15:11 NKJV).

Then there are the words of Nehemiah. He reveals a powerful principle. Nehemiah 8:10 (NKJV) states, "Do not sorrow, for the joy of the Lord is our strength."

The people had heard God's Word read and were deeply convicted. They wept and mourned at the sound of the law. But Nehemiah revealed an essential truth when speaking to broken people. He told them to go home and celebrate, reminding them, "The joy of the Lord is our strength." In other words, if the enemy takes your joy, he gets your strength. Joy and strength go hand in hand. This principle explains why the enemy loves to discourage and depress with his lies. He gets your strength by stealing your joy.

Notice how the book of Acts connects the Holy Spirit and joy. Acts 13:50–52 (NKJV) says,

> But the Jews stirred up the devout and prominent women and the chief men of the city, raised up persecution against Paul and Barnabas, and expelled them from their region. But they shook off the dust from their feet against them, and came to Iconium. And the disciples were filled with joy and with the Holy Spirit.

In the face of severe persecution and rejection, Paul and Barnabas did not lose joy. The Jews, devout and prominent women, and chief men of the city did not give Paul and Barnabas joy. It was a gift from God. Their worldly power may have given them authority to "expel them from their region," but it did not provide them with the ability to rob Paul and Barnabas of their joy.

Then Paul lists peace. Everyone wants peace. The opposite of peace is anxiety and stress. I remember hearing this quote: "Most people live in quiet desperation." I have found that to be true. The strength that comes with peace is invaluable. A tranquil heart is as rare as diamonds and much more valuable. And yet, Jesus came that we may have peace in this turbulent, pain-filled, sin-stricken world. Look closely at Jesus's teaching in John 14:25–27 (NKJV):

> "These things I have spoken to you while being present with you. But the Helper, the Holy Spirit, whom the Father will send in My name, He will teach you all things, and bring to your remembrance all things that I said to you. Peace I leave with you, My peace I give to you; not as the world gives do I give to you. Let not your heart be troubled, neither let it be afraid."

If peace were for sale, many more would have it. But that's the point. It's not for sale. It never has been and never will be. God will not sell it to you, but He will give it to you. Now, that's a much better deal. If money brings peace, why do so many who have so much of it live with so little peace? It's true that the poorest man in the world is the man who has nothing but money. Peace is a gift from God. Jesus had it and wants to give it to us. You can receive it today, bringing unparalleled stability to your life.

Next up for Paul was longsuffering, also known as patience. Patience is a stabilizing force in the lives of those who have it. Patience, in essence, is the power to wait without worrying. Someone said, "Impatience will cost you more than patience."

There is a fragility that comes with impatience. Those who are impatient are often antsy and restless. Do you need patience today? If so, yield to the Holy Spirit. Be filled with Him and experience the supernatural strength that patience produces.

A Spirit-filled life also produces kindness. Kindness is in high demand but often in short supply. Think about it on a practical level. Kind people do seem to be much more stable in life. People who are always agitated and irritable are on edge. Followers of Jesus should consider rudeness unacceptable. Strangely, and I mean very strangely, some of the rudest people I have ever met have not been in the world but in the church. I love the church. Don't get me wrong. But my experience is what it is. I don't believe for a second that true believers in Christ can be content in their rudeness; they can't claim to be living the Spirit-filled life. Unkindness is a sure indicator of a flesh-driven life. God's Spirit produces kindness. And there's strength in kindness.

Next is goodness. It's a simple word, but it's a quality the Spirit produces in the believer's life. Who hasn't been told by a parent, teacher, or coach to be good? Most of us have. Perhaps its meaning is best captured in the words of Peter, as recorded in Acts 10:38 (NKJV): "'how God anointed Jesus of Nazareth with the Holy Spirit and with power, who went about doing good and healing all who were oppressed by the devil, for God was with Him.'"

Even here, you can see the connection between the Holy Spirit and goodness. Goodness involves action, doing the right thing for the right reason.

The good deeds of followers of Jesus bring Him glory. Read this slowly. You are not saved because of your goodness, but God can get great glory from your good deeds. Jesus said, "Let your light so shine before men, that they may see your good works and glorify your Father in heaven" (Matthew 5:16 NKJV).

Paul then mentions faithfulness. This word is closely connected to dependability. Another word closely linked to faithfulness is constancy. Faithful people are reliable. You can depend on them. Wouldn't you love to be described as faithful, trustworthy, dependable, constant, and reliable?

Next up is gentleness. Sadly, many consider gentleness as a weakness. The gentle do not lack strength at all. I have heard gentleness as being like steel wrapped in velvet. That should give you a good mental image of kindness and gentleness. So often, rude and obnoxious people overcompensate for their deep insecurities.

Lastly, Paul mentions self-control. Is anyone more stable in life than one with self-control? This fruit is essential to living a windproof life. Self-control enables us to have power over fleshly impulses. It's worth noting that self-control is possible because of the power of the Spirit inside us. The Holy Spirit enables us to overcome the fleshly impulses we all experience. You don't have to be mastered by feelings. Someone once said, "We are believers, not feelers." But those who lack self-control are often controlled and led by their feelings. The Proverb writer wrote, "A person without self-control is like a city with broken-down walls" (Proverbs 25:28 NLT).

Windproof Challenge:
One word to challenge you concerning the Holy Spirit comes to mind: yield. Yield means "to give way." It's an act of the will and a necessity to walk in the fullness of the Holy Spirit. Maybe you feel the need to be in control of your life. Yielding to the Holy Spirit places Him in control. And you will

find your life is more stable and secure when you have yielded and surrendered to Him.

Take another look at Paul's fruit list from Galatians 5:22–23: love, joy, peace, longsuffering, kindness, goodness, faithfulness, gentleness, and self-control. Who doesn't want those characteristics in life? And the best news is none of these are for sale. But you can have them by trusting Christ and yielding to the Holy Spirit. Be filled with the Spirit, and you will live a windproof life.

8

FOCUS

I was speaking at a men's event in Odessa, Texas, and during a break, I had a fascinating conversation with a former Major League baseball player. Of course, I am amazed by the skill of any professional athlete, but I have always wondered about the difference between a player who makes it to the big leagues and one who doesn't. So given this unique opportunity to talk to a former Red Sox player, I asked, "What is the difference between guys who make it and those who don't?"

Granted, there are multiple answers to such a question. Injuries and internal politics are likely contributors, but his response still amazes me. He said, "Now, you will not believe me when I tell you this, but there were days I could see the letters on a fastball." In other words, keen eyesight and the discipline to focus are significant factors in making it to the Major League.

Focus is not only crucial in sports; it is essential to living a windproof life. Remember, we can do nothing to avoid all the storms in life. The real question is, are we prepared? And one way to prepare and weather the rainy and windy days is to live a life of focus on Jesus. When we lose focus, we tend to drift. And we never drift to good places.

The writer of Hebrews certainly understood the importance of focusing on the Lord. He wrote,

> Therefore we also, since we are surrounded by so great a cloud of witnesses, let us lay aside every weight, and the sin which so easily ensnares *us*, and let us run with endurance the race that is set before us, looking unto Jesus, the author and finisher of *our* faith, who for the joy that was set before Him endured the cross, despising the shame, and has sat down at the right hand of the throne of God. (Hebrews 12:1–2 NKJV)

The writer uses a marathon as a metaphor for life. He paints the picture of an athlete running a race in a stadium surrounded by fans. The runner must set aside anything that will cause resistance and keep him from running at maximum speed.

The passage then deals with the runner's focus. He writes, "Looking unto Jesus." In other words, the runner's focal point is essential, and to run the race of life effectively, the runner's eyes must be fixed on the right person—and that is unquestionably Jesus!

Distraction is the enemy's goal because focus is necessary for victorious living. He is the master of distraction. And while

I do not like to give the devil and his minions any credit, they are not ignorant. Evil, yes; ignorant, no. He is crafty, subtle, and cunning. And the last thing he wants you to do is to fix your eyes on Jesus. He knows when that happens, victory results.

The best example of this principle is the story of Peter walking on water. The Bible says, "And when He had sent the multitudes away, He went up on the mountain by Himself to pray. Now when evening came, He was alone there. But the boat was now in the middle of the sea, tossed by the waves, for the wind was contrary" (Matthew 14:23–24 NKJV).

The disciples were in a difficult place: wind and waves were taking their toll on the boat. But Jesus was on the way. His arrival brought about one of the greatest miracles mentioned in the Bible. Jesus approached the fear-stricken disciples with these words: "Be of good cheer! It is I; do not be afraid" (Matthew 14:27 NKJV).

In a storm, nothing is more valuable than the presence of Jesus. It must have been a great relief for the disciples to hear Jesus say, "It is I," but Peter took things a little further than the other disciples. That should not be surprising. "And Peter answered Him and said, 'Lord, if it is You, command me to come to You on the water'" (Matthew 14:28 NKJV).

You talk about a bold request! We should be so bold in prayer that only God can get the glory when the answer comes. That's what Peter did. Due to the magnitude of his request, Peter could not take credit when Jesus answered. Look closely at what scripture says happened: "So He said, 'Come.' And when Peter had come down out of the boat, he walked on the water to go to Jesus" (Matthew 14:29 NKJV).

So far, so good. Peter is walking on water. It's a miracle. And Peter is the only one experiencing it. The other disciples perceive it, but only Peter experiences the miracle.

This is an excellent place to chase a little rabbit. Do you ever get tired of hearing about all Jesus is doing in the lives of others without any stories of your own to share? Don't get me wrong. I love to listen to testimonies, but I also love to share personal stories of God's faithfulness. Peter was the only one to walk on water that day. Was it available to others? I believe it was had they had the faith to ask as Peter did. But they were left watching Peter experience the miraculous.

Peter walked on the water that had terrorized him and his friends just moments before. But it was a brief walk. And the problem was not his legs nor the raging sea. Instead, he became distracted. His eyes shifted, and down he went. "But when he saw that the wind *was* boisterous, he was afraid; and beginning to sink he cried out, saying, 'Lord, save me!'" (Matthew 14:30 NKJV).

And Jesus did save him. But why did Peter begin to sink? What happened? Distraction happened. His eyes shifted. He lost focus. And mercifully, Jesus rescued him.

This story is loaded with helpful principles, so let's focus. As is the case so often, Peter was moving forward, walking on water, but a distraction derailed him. The truth of this story is played out repeatedly in the lives of believers. His stability on the windy sea was lost when he, by choice, lost focus. He was windproof until he focused on the problem rather than the solution, Jesus.

I hope that many who have lost focus will pick this book up. It would be a great blessing for the words in this chapter to help some regain focus on the Lord. As a pastor, I have seen so many come and go. The reasons for this vary. But without question, a significant contributing factor in lives that derailed is simply the loss of focus. Eyes once firmly fixed on Jesus shifted, and the decline began.

Let's go back to my baseball friend I mentioned at the opening of this chapter. Imagine him stepping up to the plate, thousands of fans in the stadium, the smell of popcorn in the air, and the opposing pitcher on the mound. At that moment, with all the things that could capture his attention, all that matters is a little round ball that weighs approximately five ounces. If he looks at anything else, he has no chance of succeeding. Amid all the distractions, a ball about nine inches in circumference must hold his attention. A baseball traveling ninety miles an hour is hard enough to hit if you can see it. It is impossible to hit if you are looking at anything else. This simple illustration summarizes why many people are unstable and lack consistency in their walk with Christ. It boils down to the inability, or unwillingness, to focus on the Lord for any substantial amount of time.

You may be spiritually stuck because something or someone has distracted you. I wish you could see all God wants to do with and through your life. But a distraction(s) is blocking the view for too many.

Distractions often come in the form of temptation. Take David, for instance. The beloved king and psalmist of Israel looked down and saw Bathsheba. At that moment, and perhaps before, he was distracted from the Lord. He fixed his sights on her. His desire for her consumed him and led to one of the saddest stories in the Bible. But it all began with his eyes becoming fixed on her. He lost sight of God (spiritually) as he fixed his gaze on Bathsheba (physically), another man's wife. This distraction proved very costly.

When I teach on focus, I often spread my hands open and hold up each index finger. I then say, "Focus on both of my index fingers." I always quickly say, "You can't." This inevitably gets the attention of many men in the audience. They take it as a challenge. But in all the years I have done this, I have never had one come to me and say he had been able to focus on both. Do you know why? Because it is not possible. In the same way, you cannot focus on the Lord and something/someone else.

So many focus on their problems. I remember hearing John Maxwell say at a conference, "All God's people got problems." Of course, he was saying it humorously, but it's true. He was right. In this world, there are more than enough problems to go around. A buddy of mine called me many years ago. After a brief exchange, he said, "I got more problems than a math book!" We can all relate to him at times.

The good news is that we do not have to focus on our problems. That does not mean we are not aware of them, nor does it mean we are in denial. Instead, our focus can remain on Jesus amid it all. People who only want to focus on and highlight their problems every time you are around them are draining. Sometimes, we all need to share our burdens and pain with a friend or counselor, but that is not the same as always being consumed by problems. Just because someone does not tell you they are having trouble does not mean they are not. It could mean problems do not consume them.

Consider Jesus's well-known teaching on anxiety and stress. He reminds the listeners that stress results from seeking the wrong thing. He said, "Therefore do not worry, saying, 'What shall we eat? or What shall we drink? or What shall we wear?' For after all these things the Gentiles seek" (Matthew 6:31–32 NKJV).

Notice that Jesus emphasizes that the problem is in what the Gentiles seek. They were seeking the wrong things, and it resulted in stress. So according to Jesus, what is the solution to stress and anxiety? Is it making more money? Getting more stuff? No. We all know too many people with lots of stuff but no peace. Jesus taught that stress and anxiety result from misplaced priorities. But peace results from seeking first—focusing—on the Lord. "But seek first the kingdom of God and His righteousness, and all these things shall be added to you" (Matthew 6:33 NKJV).

One of the greatest blessings in life is having the ability to choose what we focus our spiritual eyes on. We can seek first whatever or whomever we want. No matter what happens, our hearts and minds can remain focused on God and the Word. Isaiah wrote, "You will keep *him* in perfect peace, *Whose* mind is stayed *on You*, Because he trusts in You" (Isaiah 26:3 NKJV).

Jesus remained focused. He never lost sight of the Father or His will. Throughout the Gospels, Jesus had a laser-like focus. This truth was captured when He was very young. After getting separated from His parents for a considerable amount of time, they found Him with the teachers in the temple. He was only twelve years old.

> Now so it was *that* after three days they found Him in the temple, sitting in the midst of the teachers, both listening to them and asking them questions. And all who heard Him were astonished at His understanding and answers. So when they saw Him, they were amazed; and His mother said to Him, "Son, why have You done this to us? Look, Your father and I have sought You anxiously." And He said to them, "Why did you seek Me? Did you not know that I must be about My Father's business?" (Luke 2:46–49 NKJV)

If you have ever been there as a parent, you know what Mary and Joseph experienced. But Jesus's response to Mary gives us a glimpse into His focus. He reminded her that His focus was the plan and purpose of His Father. This focus would remain until years later when, from the cross, He cried, "It is finished!"

I desire this chapter to make you think about the importance of focusing on Jesus when the winds and rains of life come. We tend to shift our focus when life gets hard. We are prone to fixate on problems rather than on God. When this happens, the result is stress, discouragement, fear, and even depression. You may have never considered how important the object of your focus is.

We live in an age of distractions. Technological devices and social media have changed the game. The advances of the past forty years have exceeded what most thought possible. Indeed, some saw it coming, but not most. And while the technology of the day has its advantages, I believe it is taking its toll on our ability to focus on what's important.

Screen time refers to how much time a person spends focusing on a screen. This term was unknown two hundred years ago. In 2022, a person's average time staring at a screen was six hours and fifty-eight minutes daily. Of course, for some, this includes working in front of a computer or watching TV, but we know Facebook, Twitter, Instagram, YouTube, Snapchat, TikTok, and many more apps monopolize our time. Can one honestly say they are focused on God while spending hours daily on social media? It's an easy answer. No.

It takes high-level discipline to focus on Jesus today. Other things are constantly vying for our attention. It's the age of pings, dings, and rings. Each refers to sound made by devices that notify us of something or someone demanding our attention. While these are known as notifications, they could also be called distractions. A phone used to be a device on your wall or desk to communicate verbally. Not anymore.

The modern telephone, designed to pocket 24/7 easily, is often used less for verbal communication than any other form and, for that reason, is potentially highly distracting.

Let's travel back in time. Imagine Paul, a captive in a Roman prison for obeying God. Unsure of his future, he penned the words to the beloved believers in Philippi that remind us of Paul's focus. Paul did not seem shaken at all by his circumstances. The winds of severe persecution could not blow away his contagious joy.

Like many, Paul knew what it was like to be in the cold hand of vain religion. He was a Hebrew of Hebrews and a Pharisee (Philippians 3:5), the cream of the crop, top dog, king of the mountain (you get the picture). But the law-based religion Saul of Tarsus had practiced knew nothing of a genuine relationship with God. So when Paul met Jesus on the Damascus Road, he traded legalistic religion for a vibrant relationship. Jesus did not become part of his life. Instead, he *became* Paul's life. "For to me, to live *is* Christ, and to die *is* gain" (Philippians 1:21 NKJV).

This simple verse tells us the secret to Paul's stability, peace, and joy even while in prison: focus.

Think about it. Everyone is living for something or someone. Paul said, "To live *is* Christ." Everyone has something to fill that blank space: "To live is _____." What would you place in that blank today? What or who is at the center of your life? Jesus was the focus of Paul's life even in prison.

Is Jesus an *addition* to your life or your life? There is a difference. And you will never possess the abundant life God has for you if Jesus is simply a part of your life. You will only experience the glorious benefits of knowing Him when He is at the center. This was one of Paul's secrets to remaining stable in shaky times. Paul modeled focus. He lived, literally, the Christ life. And you can too.

Those easily distracted forfeit stability. Problems, people, and especially problem people, can steal your focus. Few stories in the Bible illustrate the importance of maintaining one's focus on the Lord more than David and Goliath.

I wrote a short book, *From Cheese Carrier to Champion*, many years ago. David's focus in his battle with Goliath has always struck me. Everyone but David seemed consumed with the imposing giant. The soldiers were full of fear. The Bible says,

> And all the men of Israel, when they saw the man, fled from him and were dreadfully afraid. So the men of Israel said, "Have you seen this man who has come up? Surely he has come up to defy Israel; and it shall be *that* the man who kills him the king will enrich with great riches, will give him his daughter, and give him his father's house exemption *from taxes* in Israel." (1 Samuel 17:24–25 NKJV)

Later, King Saul said to David, "You are not able to go against this Philistine to fight with him; for you *are* a youth, and he a man of war from his youth" (1 Samuel 17:33 NKJV).

Saul and the soldiers were consumed with Goliath. They focused on the problem. Essentially, they feared Goliath because they focused on him. But along came David.

In response to Saul's dim outlook, David responded. Look at 1 Samuel 17:37 (NKJV): "Moreover David said, 'The Lord, who delivered me from the paw of the lion and from the paw of the bear, He will deliver me from the hand of this Philistine.' And Saul said to David, 'Go, and the Lord be with you!'"

Look at David's focus. He was aware of Goliath but focused on God. David did not fear Goliath partly because he did not focus on him. Instead, David focused on the God of Israel, who had shown Himself faithful to the young shepherd boy. David did not have the skills or equipment of the trained soldiers, but the soldiers did not have the faith and focus of David. And in the end, David's focus on the Lord was much more important than armor and experience. He defeated Goliath because he focused on God. He was aware of the arrogant giant, but God was his focus.

No matter what people physically focus on, they can still see many objects in their peripheral vision. The problem is, spiritually speaking, many of us focus on our Goliath and see God in our periphery. Instead, like David, we should focus on the Lord and see our problems in our periphery. There is a significant difference.

I would like to share one last story concerning focus, one I briefly mentioned in the chapter on prayer. The story centers around a man named Jehoshaphat. He was the fourth king of Judah. This little-known king faced a big crisis; we can learn from his response. Second Chronicles 20:1–2 (NKJV) says,

> It happened after this *that* the people of Moab with the people of Ammon, and *others* with them besides the Ammonites, came to battle against Jehoshaphat. Then some came and told Jehoshaphat, saying, "A great multitude is coming against you from beyond the sea, and from Syria; and they are in Hazazon Tamar (which is En Gedi)."

Jehoshaphat received terrible news. A band of armies had allied and made him and Judah their target. I love this story because we have Jehoshaphat's initial and ultimate response: "And Jehoshaphat feared, and set himself to seek the Lord, and proclaimed a fast throughout all Judah" (2 Chronicles 20:3 NKJV).

Initially, the Bible says, "And Jehoshaphat feared." The news of multiple enemies coming against him brought fear. But what did he do next? That's the big question. The fear he felt prompted him to regain focus. The Bible says that upon feeling fear, he "set himself to seek the Lord, and proclaimed a fast throughout all Judah." He heard the news, felt the fear, and took action to focus on the Lord.

Our problem is that we allow fear to enter and take up residence. The problem (the alliance of enemies in Jehoshaphat's case) often consumes our minds. We become preoccupied with the problem rather than with the One who can help us. As a result, a spirit of fear takes over, which becomes spiritually, mentally, and emotionally debilitating. Fear will not only stick around if you let it; it will take over.

But in my opinion, Jehoshaphat gives us one of the best Bible lessons on dealing with potentially distracting and devastating news. Sure, we all have the choice to become consumed with problems in whatever form they may come. For example, financial and relational issues consume many minds; some whose minds are cluttered with problems are reading this book. A problem may have you so preoccupied that focusing on Christ seems impossible.

Ultimately, what or who you focus on is your choice. If David could maintain focus on God while standing before a giant over nine feet tall, you can focus on Jesus no matter what giant you are facing. If Paul, in prison, kept Jesus at the center of his life while being persecuted, so can you. Let's revisit Jehoshaphat before closing. He turned his attention to the Lord. He could have focused on the size of the collective army coming against him. Fear could have paralyzed him. But instead, he fixed his eyes on the Lord. Second Chronicles 20:12 (NKJV) reveals part of his prayer: "O our God, will You not judge them? For we have no power against this great multitude that is coming against us; nor do we know what to do, but our eyes *are* upon You."

Look again at the last words: "But our eyes *are* upon You." That's essential to living a windproof life. From an earthly standpoint, Jehoshaphat and the nation he led had no chance. So he turned his eyes to heaven. And here again is the good news. So can you. You can focus on the Lord no matter what or who you face. Of course, there will always be the option to be problem-focused, but that option is costly.

In 1922, Helen Lammel wrote a beautiful song inspired by a missionary named Lilias Trotter. This song has touched the hearts of many throughout the world. Trotter's poem, "Focussed: A Story and a Song," inspired the song. Due to space, I will only share one line of the poetry and a portion of the song it inspired. Trotter wrote, "And Satan knows the power of concentration." This line, along with the rest of the poem, led Lammel to pen these words:

> Oh soul, are you wearied and troubled?
> No light in the darkness you see?
> There's light for a look at the Savior,
> And life more abundant and free.
>
> Turn your eyes upon Jesus,
> Look full in His wonderful face,
> And the things of earth will grow strangely dim,
> In the light of His glory and grace.

Turn your eyes upon Jesus.

Windproof Challenge:
The dodo bird's extinction around 1690 marked the species' permanent disappearance from the island of Mauritius in the Indian Ocean. Focus, metaphorically speaking, should be on the endangered species list and recognized as fast approaching extinction. There is a high price to pay when Christians and churches are not focused.

As dealt with in this chapter, the world's system and the devil have ample ammunition to distract followers of Christ. But distractions can also come in the form of hobbies and entertainment. I certainly do not want to sound like having hobbies and enjoying certain forms of entertainment are wrong. However, they can be.

Too often, good things distract us from the best. I have pastored long enough to tell you that many people have lost focus on the Lord and His church due to work, deer, fish, beaches, malls, baseball, football, and—you get the picture. In the proper place, all of these are good things. However, when they take the place of worshiping and serving the Lord, they become idols and, thus, distractions. Good things become bad things when they take the place of the main thing. Remember, your life will only be windproof when focused on Jesus. So if needed, rearrange. If anything other than Jesus tops your priority list, move it or remove it!

> We do this by keeping our eyes on Jesus, the champion who initiates and perfects our faith. Because of the joy awaiting him, he endured the cross, disregarding its shame. Now He is seated in the place of honor beside God's throne. (Hebrews 12:2 NLT)

CONCLUSION

By writing this book, I aim to help believers live prosperous and stable lives. It seems easier to sing "Victory in Jesus" than to live victoriously. Metaphorically speaking, life's landscape is littered with storms, giants, walls, mountains, and valleys. We will all face them. You can't get godly enough to be exempt from the trials of life. This fallen world is rife with pain, and we all experience our share.

Storms blow some away, and giants defeat others. Walls and mountains often stand between people and all God has for them. Valleys plummet too many blood-bought children of God into depression and hopelessness. But still, there's good news. Followers of Jesus can remain windproof no matter the power of the storm, the size of the giant, the strength of the wall, the height of the mountain, or the depth of the valley. Remember Jesus's words:

> "Therefore whoever hears these words of Mine, and does them, I will liken him to a wise man who built his house on the rock: and the rain descended, the floods came, and the winds blew and beat on that house; and it did not fall, for it was founded on the rock." (Matthew 7:24–25 NKJV)

In the Garden of Eden, Adam and Eve's disobedience brought about the onslaught of devastation we see today. But who was behind it? You guessed it: the great deceiver, Satan. There is a reason the enemy is a relentless liar. He knows that once believed, lies lead to self-destruction.

Through masterful temptation and, ultimately, sin, the devil brought instability to Adam, Eve, humanity, and even creation itself. He continues to deceive and divide today with the same strategy, bringing chaos and instability.

I believe this is why Paul uses the language he does in Ephesians. He writes, "Put on the whole armor of God, that you may be able to stand against the wiles of the devil" (Ephesians 6:11 NKJV).

Then in verses 13 and 14 of the same chapter, he writes, "Therefore take up the whole armor of God, that you may be able to withstand in the evil day, and having done all, to stand. Stand therefore, having girded your loins with the truth, having put on the breastplate of righteousness."

He uses *stand* three times and *withstand* once. The NASB translates withstand as *stand firm*. It's interpreted as *the opposite of falling* and *to place in a balance*. The enemy wants you to fall, to live unbalanced lives, wavering and faltering.

Contrast this with God's will for your life as a believer:

> He only *is* my rock and
> my salvation;
> *He is* my defense;
> I shall not be greatly moved. (Psalm 62:2 NKJV)

> He also brought me up
> out of a horrible pit,
> Out of the miry clay,
> And set my feet upon a rock,

And established my steps. (Psalm 40:2 NKJV)

Here is one of my favorites: "He makes me as surefooted as a deer, Enabling me to stand on mountain heights" (Psalm 18:33 NLT).

So here's my closing questions: Do you want to live a stable life in an unstable world? Do you want to stand? I believe I am correct to assume everyone answers yes. We all desire stability in a dangerous world with a real foe who aims to steal, kill, and destroy (John 10:10). You can live a stable, victorious life. As the winds of the world inevitably blow your way, Jesus is an anchor that always holds. Hebrews 6:19 (NLT) states, "This hope is a strong and trustworthy anchor for our souls. It leads us through the curtain into God's inner sanctuary."

You can't straddle the spiritual fence and remain surefooted. James wrote,

> If any of you lacks wisdom, let him ask of God, who gives to all liberally and without reproach, and it will be given to him. But let him ask in faith, with no doubting, for he who doubts is like a wave in the sea driven and tossed by the wind. For let not that man suppose that he will receive anything from the Lord; *he is* a double-minded man, unstable in all his ways. (James 1:5–8 NKJV)

These verses reveal that doubt and double-mindedness significantly contribute to life on sinking sand. So don't doubt and waver. Instead,

- trust Jesus as Savior,
- constantly pray,

- generously give,
- always forgive,
- remain humble,
- know God's love for you, love God, and love people,
- walk in the Spirit, and
- stay focused.

And you, in a turbulent, topsy-turvy world, will remain windproof.

> When the whirlwind passes by,
> The wicked *is* no *more*, But the righteous *has* an everlasting foundation. (Proverbs 10:25 NKJV)

Printed in the United States
by Baker & Taylor Publisher Services